No Shame in the Game:
Releasing Your Soul So Your Spirit Can Soar

By Dr. Kasim Ali Sidney Jones

Dr. Kasim Ali Sidney Jones

Copyright © 2016 Dr. Kasim Ali Sidney Jones

All rights reserved.

ISBN-13: 978-1-7370905-1-9 (Paperback)
ISBN-13: 978-1-7370905-0-2 (Hard Cover)

DEDICATION

To those who struggle with shame, which may be all of us, and are struggling to find in your life.

Dr. Kasim Ali Sidney Jones

No Shame in the Game

Table of Contents

Dedication……………………………………………………………iii

Acknowledgments…………………………………………………vii

Introduction………………………………………………………… viii

Part One: The Cost of Shame

What is Shame?………………………………………………………2

    Ezra: The Cost of Racial Prejudice……………………5

    Alice: The Cost of Sexual Abuse… ………………….10

    Cissy: Striving for Perfection………………………….15

    Danny: Need for Control/Striving for Power……….18

    Isn't It A Shame?………………………………………….20

    It Gets in the Way………………………………………..25

Part Two: The Price Paid for Shame

    The Wonderful Counselor……………………………….31

    The Lowest of Highs: Nicodemus…………………….31

    He Who Knows: The Samaritan Woman at the Well….34

    Score the Final Point: The Lame Man…………………38

Part Three: Living with Significance

    What Do You Mean?……………………………………..42

Meaning as It Is Meant to Be..........................46

Meant to Move Forward................................53

Part Four: Making Sense of It All................................58

Epilogue..63

About the Author..66

References..68

ACKNOWLEDGEMENTS

I give all the honor, the glory and the praise to God for all of the things God has done in my life. None of these things—not one thing—would have been possible if it had not been for the Lord on my side.

To my family, friends and those who have studied, researched, written about, and dedicated their lives to the subject matter presented in this book.

Dr. Kasim Ali Sidney Jones

Introduction

Being human is a phenomenon that is undergirded by emotions. Love and hate play against one another with love being the greater of the two. In the Christian tradition, we are taught that God is love and love is God (1 John 4:8). We are to strive to love one another as God loves us. This agape love is unconditional and is without limits. It is here that God accepts us for who we are even when others—including ourselves—do not. For many, this is a great challenge for countless reasons. Be it our upbringings or life experiences, loving others—including ourselves—requires stretching and testing who we believe we are. Interestingly enough, our memories and emotive capabilities can present roadblocks that hold us captive, not allowing us to move on. Unfortunately, we run the risk of becoming complacent in where we are because we are afraid to move forward because we *remember* what was done in the past. We live and move in the past.

As I write these words and think about where I am at this point of my life, I had to come to grips with how my emotions have wreaked havoc in my life. This is a pivotal juncture in my life because I had to look at some of the messages I have received thus far and consider how they fit in. What makes this feat so intense is that I had to consider challenging some of those messages. I turned 40 years young on October 11th, 2011, and this was an occasion I looked forward to almost all of my life. As my 40th birthday approached, strange things started happening, even though there were many wonderful things occurring as well. I tried lifting up the positive things in my life, like earning a doctoral degree and being gainfully employed. And the, all of a sudden, I ran out of money to pay the last installment of my tuition for school, and the agency I was working for abruptly closed their doors without paying me for the services rendered for a couple of months. All of this overwhelmed me to the point where I began to weep at the slightest things or when least expected. This behavior went against one of the messages I received as a child: "Real men don't cry." Initially, I was embarrassed because crying caused me to question my own "manhood" and what I had seen as a child. I had to come to grips with the reality that crying and tears are helpful in order to maintain my emotional and psychological wellbeing and stability.

No Shame in the Game

This book is a God-inspired answer to my prayers for understanding and comfort. I wanted to know that I would be okay, even though it seemed as if things were falling apart around me. My desire was to receive conformation from God that all of my hard work and education was not for naught. Most of all, I just wanted to do something that would help others and make a difference in the world. First, I had to rest and replenish myself. And then, God spoke: "Sit down and write." Naturally, my flesh began asking questions: Write about what? Where do I start? What will I write that will make a difference in someone else's life? To be totally honest, I was tired of writing. After all, I had worked on my dissertation for a year-and-a-half and really was not in the mood to write extensively just yet. Obediently, I prepared myself and started getting myself in the position to hear from God in this regard. One day a friend of mine asked, "How do you know when God is speaking to you?" My immediate response was: "When thoughts and/or ideas come to my mind that are not my own." I felt comfortable with sharing this with someone other than myself for a change. "Why is that?" you may ask. My response was a clear indication of my spiritual growth and maturation; thus, again, bringing down an emotional defense that held me down for most of my life—shame. Therefore, I had to settle down and receive the words, ideas, and the concepts from God for this endeavor.

In *No Shame in the Game*, I set out to accomplish several things: 1) to provide operational definitions of shame, 2) to talk about some of the origins of shame, and 3) to discuss some of the destructive properties that shame can have over our lives. *No Shame in the Game* contains intellectual and biblical components to inspire us to understand what Romans 8: 1 – 17 is calling us to grasp, comprehend, and ultimately, live. *No Shame in the Game* also demonstrates how Jesus the Christ continues to guide us to liberty from the grips of shame, while Logotherapy provides a viable method that can assist us in our quest to escape shame's lethal grip.

Shame is an imposing emotion and it can act as a blocking agent in our lives. It is our job to see it for what it is, and how it affects our physical, psychological, and emotional selves. The promising Word of God states so boldly and eloquently declared in Romans 8, "So now there is no condemnation for those who belong to Christ Jesus. For the power of the life-giving Spirit has freed you through Christ Jesus from the power of sin that leads to death" (vv. 1 -2, *New Living Translation*). Living under the crushing weight of shame, whether it is self-imposed or inflected by others, can rob us of our joy and the freedom that was given through Christ Jesus. Certainly, in some cases, shame can act as our conscious, alerting us to decipher when something may be wrong. But shame is also something that restricts us from doing what we have been created to do. Therefore, the condemnation that Paul spoke of in the passage mentioned above is also interpreted as guilt and shame. We are free from these things because of the love of God through Jesus the Christ.

    May God lead and guide all of us through the valleys as we approach restoration and deliverance from shame.

K.A S. J.

November 2011

Hiram, GA

Dr. Kasim Ali Sidney Jones

Part One:

The Cost of Shame

"When Jesus noticed that all who had come to the dinner were trying to sit near the head of the table, he gave them this advice: 'If you are invited to a wedding feast, don't always head for the best seat. What if someone more respected than you has also been invited? The host will say, 'Let this person sit here instead?' Then you will be embarrassed (ashamed) and will have to take whatever seat is left at the foot of the table! Do this instead—sit at the foot of the table. Then when your host sees you, he will come and say, 'Friend, we have a better place than this for you! Then you will be honored in front of all the other guests. For the proud will be humbled, but the humble will be honored'."

Luke 14: 7 – 11 (*New Living Translation*)

"And so, since they did not see fit to acknowledge God or approve of Him *or* consider Him worth the knowing, God gave them over to a base *and* condemned mind to do things not proper *or* decent *but* loathsome. Until they were filled (permeated and saturated) with every kind of unrighteousness, iniquity, grasping and covetous greed, and malice. [They were] full of envy *and* jealousy, murder, strife, deceit *and* treachery, ill will *and* cruel way. [They were] secret backbiters and gossipers, slanderers, hateful to *and* hating God, full of insolence, arrogance, [and] boasting; inventors of new forms of evil, disobedient *and* undutiful to parents. [They were] without understanding, conscienceless *and* faithless, heartless *and* loveless [and] merciless. Though they are fully aware of God's righteous decree that those who do such things deserve to die, they not only do them themselves but approve *and* applaud others who practice them."

Romans 1: 28 – 32 (*The Amplified Bible*)

What Is Shame?

What is shame, and why is it so hard to deal with? These are critical questions because they seek to unravel a number of misunderstandings about what we have been taught about who we are and what we believe now. Getting to the root of such a notion has the potential to begin the quest towards personal freedom and management of our thoughts and feelings regarding shame and its place in our lives. By achieving such a daring deed, we can free ourselves from a lot of negativity and sort out our thoughts and feelings about shame. This process has to begin with a working definition of what shame really is.

Shame has been defined and discussed in a number of ways. In her book entitled, *Released from Shame*, Wilson (1990) wrote the following:

> *Shame is a strong sense of being uniquely and hopelessly different and less than other human beings.* When you experience shame, you feel isolated and alienated from others. It is as if you are standing alone on one side of a broken bridge while everyone else in the world stares at you from the other side (p. 25, containing an insert from Kaufman, 1985; emphasis mine).

In this sense, shame forces one to feel separated from the rest of the world, while feeling inadequate at the same time. There is a valuable note to be made about the word *force*. Force is having something or someone to move you, even when you do not want to be moved. Force is, as defined by *The American Heritage College Dictionary* (1997), the "Power made operative against resistance, exertion" (p. 531). Hawkins (1998) added that

> Force always creates counterforce; its effect is to polarize rather than unify. Polarization always implies conflict; its cost, therefore, is always high. Because force incites polarization, *it inevitably produces a win/lose dichotomy; and because somebody always loses, enemies are created; constantly faced with enemies, force requires constant defense.* Defensiveness is invariably costly... Force is concrete, literal, and arguable. It requires proof and

support (p. 133, emphasis mine).

Because force, by nature, oftentimes creates win/lose dichotomies in its essence, and shame becomes a factor upon which we feel the effects of being pushed or pulled into positions upon which we "lose"—lose control, lose meaning, and most of all, lose touch.

When operating in shame one finds no hope in reconnecting with another person nor do they feel they are worthy of such a connection with anyone. They feel as though they are unworthy of being a part of the rest of humanity and are cast aside all together. Kaufman (1996) asserted that "Shame is the affect of inferiority" (p. 16). The use of the word *affect* is very important because it is geared toward the emotional and psychological reactions of people and/or the individual, rather than things. Kaufman continued on to explain:

> *Shame reveals the inner self, exposing it to view*. The self feels exposed both to itself and to anyone else present. That exposure can be of the self *to* the self alone, or it can be of the self to others. Central to an understanding of the alienating affect is that shame can be an entirely *internal* experience. No one else need be present in order for shame to be felt, but when others are present shame is an impediment to further communication... In the midst of shame, the attention turns inward, thereby generating the torment of self-consciousness. Sudden unexpected exposure, coupled with binding inner scrutiny, characterize the essential nature of the affect of shame. *Whether all eyes are upon us or only our own, we feel fundamentally deficient as individuals, diseased, defective*. To live with shame is to experience the very experience the very essence or heart of the self as wanting. Shame is inevitably alienating, isolating, and deeply disturbed. (p. 17, emphasis mine).

Kaufman's explanation of shame says that when we experience shame we feel that there is something within ourselves that is defective and can be seen by others; therefore, causing us to want to simply vanish. Lewis (1995) supported this view by saying, "Shame can be defined simply as the feeling we have when we evaluate our actions, feelings, or behavior, and conclude that we have done wrong. It encompasses the *whole of ourselves;* it generates a wish to hide, to disappear, or even to die" (p. 2, emphasis mine). Shame, in this sense, is counterproductive because it leads to a person being highly critical of one's self, and not being able to see how shame can act as a regulator of our actions, thoughts, feelings, and/or behavior. Allender (2008) succinctly surmised that

> Shame is a silent killer, much the way that high blood pressure is a quiet, symptom-free destroyer. Fortunately, shame has a set of symptoms that can be discerned, once the eyes are open to its presence and operation. But like heart disease, it is easy to ignore the problem or to mislabel it as heartburn or a minor chest pain. ...Shame has the power to take our breath away and replace it with the stale air of condemnation and disgust. ...Unlike other feelings that relinquish some of their power by putting words to the inner sensation, shame has the propensity to increase in intensity when it is first acknowledged. For that reason, shame is a shameful topic, one that most people would prefer to ignore (pp. 59, 60).

I looked at the Serenity Prayer (attributed to *Reinhold Niebuhr (1892-1971)* a little closer to help me cope during a challenging time in my life. Several events transpired that I had no control over and I briefly looked at myself to see if I had anything to do with how they unfolded. The opening line says, "God, give us grace to accept with serenity the things that cannot be changed...." How powerful is this phrase? I thought some of those situations were my fault, but I found that they were not. This line says there are things in our lives and in the world that are beyond our control. So, when events that are beyond our control do happen, we must accept them as they are, not for what we did or did not do. Lewis (1995) astutely asserted that "Shame is related to guilt, pride, and hubris [arrogance], all of which also require self-awareness. Shame bares narcissism..." (p. 2). Narcissism is, by definition, an "excessive love or admiration of oneself" (*The American Heritage College Dictionary*, 1997, p. 906). However, what appears to be narcissism, a disproportionate love of oneself, becomes a part of the individual's "identity script" (Kaufman, 1996), where one's "Identity is the conscious experience of that self together with the active, living relationship the self comes to have with the self" (p. 101). In other words, a person might take "love of themselves" to an extreme in order to mask or cover the shame they had experienced in their lifetime to prevent similar experiences from occurring again. What appears to be narcissism from the outset may be a byproduct of shame and/or self-loathing, which allows the individual to negatively set themselves apart from others. Therefore, the Serenity Prayer encourages us to look beyond the things we do not have influence or power over and accept them for what they are—a part of our individual journey.

Ezra: The Cost of Racial Prejudice

Ezra is a 28-year-old, African American male, who was reared and educated in the Northeastern region of America. He works for a prominent computer software company and is pursuing a doctoral degree in Business Administration. Ezra received a promotion as a regional supervisor. He and his young family relocated to a Southern state roughly five years ago after working with this company for approximately three years after completing his undergraduate studies. Ezra chose the state to which he and his family moved to because it was where their families originated from over one hundred years ago. Through the years, he often heard stories about how his older family members had been mistreated in the south, but he rarely learned of the outcomes or their reactions to those occurrences. When Ezra asked questions as a child, he was told: "Not now." "We'll explain when you're older." "I don't want to talk about that now. It was so long ago." These incomplete family stories planted the seeds for inner struggles that would manifest as Ezra matured into adulthood.

As Ezra grew older, he realized his upbringing was filled with contradictions and missing information. Ezra often shared, "I was taught people are people, regardless of their skin color," even though there was a lot of mistrust of White people in his family. Upon graduating from high school, Ezra decided to attend a predominately white university in the Northeastern region of the country, where he majored in Computer Science. "Education is very important in my family," and he was encouraged to obtain "as much education as you can." In doing so, Ezra received many opportunities to interact with people from diverse nationalities, religious backgrounds, and races. Ezra began to realize there were a lot of details missing from his family's stories as discussions of racial heritage and sensitivity arose in some of his classes. On a number of occasions, he found himself feeling angry, embarrassed and frustrated. Ezra began showing signs of perfectionism in his studies. His interactions with his peers and instructors became strained and he was becoming more and more belligerent. Ezra immersed himself deeply into African American history and became disgruntle when asked to explain his personal and/or familial involvement during critical moments in American history.

After a number of verbal tirades, Ezra was referred to the campus counselor to explore and process some of his feelings regarding his family's history and his anger. Ezra agreed to participate in the therapeutic process, because he acknowledged a change in his behavior and attitude lately. Initially, he could not identify the source of his discontent because his thoughts and feelings were muddled in confusion and inept. When the campus counselor challenged Ezra with the possibility that he had been socialized within a racially prejudiced family system, he became indignant and verbally combative. He denied being a "bigot because I am Black." The campus counselor pressed Ezra further to consider how being Black and having been reared by family members who were reared in the "Jim Crow" South during the 1940s, 1950s and 1960s affected him. He firmly declared: "I was taught to treat people the same, regardless of their skin color." The campus counselor graciously encouraged Ezra to give thought to his childhood socialization and what he experienced in his adulthood thus far.

Ezra continued to meet with the campus counselor for several months. He discovered that he truly did not agree with the assimilative attitude he was exposed to as a child and an adolescent. As Ezra learned of the history of African Americans, he felt that "we [African Americans] are expected to change, while others [from different nationalities and ethnic backgrounds] keep on doing the same thing they have been doing for centuries." Ezra surmised that he felt as if he was being pressured to "be like other people when we [African Americans] have our own positive traits to be proud of." Ezra stated he believed this could be where his frustrations and anger came from. He also felt ashamed of his family's shame. Ezra felt that their not telling him the complete stories of his family's struggles and achievements "was the start of all of this." He also said, "Sure, there are some [family members] who made it, and live successful lives, but what about their struggles to get there. That's the important part that's missing."

The root of Ezra's frustrations was linked to his feelings of being forced to assimilate into other groups around him. Allport (1979) stated:

> This process may underlie assimilationist strivings and be factor that leads the individual to lose himself totally in the dominant group as soon as his level of possessions, customs, and speech makes him indistinguishable from the majority. But more mysterious are the cases where the individual is hopelessly barred from assimilation and yet mentally identifies himself with the practices, outlook, and prejudices of the dominant group (pp. 150 – 151).

Unconsciously, Ezra may have experienced what his family members were exposed to in the past through their stories. This phenomenon is called internalization of shame— "the self internalizes, and so reproduces, its own experience is central to how the self actually functions and develops" (Kaufman, 1996, p. 57). Ezra's distress was connected to the partial stories he heard from his older family members, their facial expressions, and their emotionality that he perceived as negative and traumatic. "It is through *imagery* (encompassing visual, auditory, and kinesthetic dimensions) that the self internalizes experience. What is internalized are images or scenes that have become imprinted with affect" (p. 57). Although Ezra did not experience what his older relatives had first-handedly, he was aware of the messages that were conveyed that included shame-filled features due to his family's experiences. Wilson (1990) skillfully illustrated how shame can be passed from generation to generation in the following statement:

> ...you believed that their unrealistic expectations of you actually were based on the reality that "good" children are *perfect* children without developmental limitations and legitimate childhood need. These *perfect* children would be able to *perfectly* please your parents because these children never track mud into the house, wet the bed, get less than an A, come in second at anything, arrive late, get a speeding ticket (or divorce), or have children who do any of the above. It seemed reasonable. After all, your parents seemed perfect. And why would they expect you to be perfect if you weren't supposed to be perfect (p. 40).

In Ezra's case, his older relatives expected him to be perfectly "color blind" in his interactions with others when, in fact, they had not worked out their own issues with their past shame caused by racial prejudice and discrimination. Therefore, Ezra received contradictory teachings because he was not given a full description of where and whom he came from—a rich African American lineage and experience. From Ezra's standpoint as a young adult, his efforts to differentiate (to distinguish himself from his family members) and assimilate (to blend in with others in society) were met with shame producing actions/reactions by many individuals who were not African American. He saw this as he performed his managerial duties and in his attempts to develop social relationships with others. Ezra realized he was not fully accepted in his environment. He started making connections with the stories he had internalized from his childhood. According to Wimberly (1999):

> Those who live within the stigmatized group internalize the negative images of the group, and those who are outside the group reenforce the negative images through their attitudes and position. Most devastating are the ways people in devalued groups internalize negative values and form their group identity. Such internalizations become the basis of personal and group identities and follow individuals and groups throughout their lives (p. 37).

Ezra's anguish began when he experienced the adverse affects of his belonging to a stigmatized group, and this incited frustration, confusion, and ultimately anger once again. These feelings were undergirded by the shame of being shamed. Ezra continued to work with the campus counselor and they began to process the effects of shame in his own life based on the slights he encountered after relocating to the south. He felt of a sense of disenchantment because he *was* taught to be color blind and was ashamed because he believed the attitudes and the actions of others had improved over the years. As Ezra continued to try to distinguish himself from his family-of-origin, he discovered that some of his experiences were similar to the ones experienced by his older relatives. He found that "Such powerful scenes are activated in subsequent experiences of shame, as the person relives the original shaming event" (Wimberly, 1999, p. 40).

Within his own adult experiences, Ezra felt alienated and ostracized within his community and from his family-of-origin. He continued to excel at work and in his studies, yet he felt socially inept. Ezra reported that his contact with his family never ended, and that his parents continued to push color blindness without him sharing his feelings of feeling like "an outsider" in his surroundings. Ezra said he did not want his parents to feel as if he was not "living up to their expectations, even though I'm a grown man with a family of my own." Without saying, Ezra did not want to risk his parents' pride and guidance by expressing his personal torment. Wimberly (1999) attributes these emotions to the family-of-origin when he explained:

> Dysfunctional families are generally families find it hard to allow family members to develop their own uniqueness and differentness; in contrast, functional families facilitate such self-differentiation. Those who insist on being themselves and developing their own unique identities are often viewed as outsiders and are seen as betrayers in dysfunctional families (p. 42).

Within the therapeutic process with the campus counselor, Ezra disclosed his family's Christian foundation. He also shared how he felt alone and/or abandoned by his parents whenever he defied their wishes as a teen. Wilson (1990) described this occurrence akin to the shepherd in Psalm 23:

> The loving care of shepherds is so legendary that we immediately respond to the image of the Good Shepherd. But imagine instead a cruel shepherd who tortures his lambs and then flings them over a cliff. This would be the same unnatural situation that occurs when overtly abusive parents thrust their children into adulthood with gaping wounds that leave the children vulnerable to further abuses.
>
> In less dramatic ways, other parents abdicate their shepherding roles by spiritually, intellectually, and/or emotionally abandoning their "lambs." This rupture in the protective parental fence leaves children exposed to foolish and dangerous wanderings (p. 57).

Ezra felt that he was unable to speak to his parents and others about his experiences for fear of being misunderstood and left alone to deal with the shame he may have felt. Eventually, he was able to acknowledge his sense of disconnection from his family's past. Ezra stated, "I can deal with the fact that there were injustices done to them, but I would like to find out how my family survived then and made it through." Many of the troubling events in Ezra's life originated from his inability to engage in healthy discussions about his family's history, which caused him shame and anguish.

Alice: The Cost of Sexual Abuse

Alice is a 59-year-old Asian American teacher, looking forward to an early retirement at the end of the current school year. Her career began when she was 21 years old—the same year she graduated from college. Alice takes great pride in helping "young people to acquire the tools needed to sculpt their futures." Apart from teaching in school, Alice also taught Sunday school since she was a teenager and was active in other auxiliaries in her church.

Alice is a devoted wife and has been happily married to her husband, Ralph, for 35 years. She and Ralph have four adult children—two daughters and two sons—and seven grandchildren. Alice lived with her family in her current home since a year after she and her husband were married, and their eldest child was born. She and Ralph had been enjoying their "empty nest" for approximately 10 years after their youngest daughter went off to college and married shortly graduation. Alice's life was built on service and she feels no regrets in doing so.

Alice's behavior began to drastically change. She seemed distant and irritable, almost isolated, inapproachable and aloof at times. Everyone who knows Alice personally and professionally noticed this sudden change in her demeanor and voiced their concerns to Ralph and to one another. The general description of Alice is: "she's straightforward, no nonsense, and truthful, even when it hurts at times. Yet she is a giving, kind, sweet person." Ralph feels that Alice is grieving her early retirement, but also feels there is something else going on. He planned to talk to Alice in order to convince her to see a therapist. Ralph believed seeing a therapist would help Alice make sense of her life, and to figure out what she can do after she retires from teaching in the school setting. Ralph decided to make this talk a family effort because he wanted Alice to feel supported not only by him but by their children as well.

Alice's children and grandchildren describe her as "a loving, caring and protective person, who will do all she can for us, others, and especially, her students." Her eldest daughter said she could recall a time when "Mom was not there for us, and she always made time for our school functions and activities." Ralph and their children all concurred that Alice "has always been present without complaining." Yet something changed. Alice seemed to be unhappy doing the things she once enjoyed. "It seems like she's lost her passion, her drive," Ralph reported. They agreed that Alice's upcoming retirement many have created a great stressor in her life, and "it is touching on something," but they are not sure of what it could be. Therefore, Alice's family decided that their intervention should be gentle yet direct, for they did not want her to feel attacked or "ganged up on."

The moment arrived when Alice and her family sat down for a much-needed discussion regarding Alice's recent behavior. Ralph and their children began the talk by telling Alice about her sweet disposition and qualities. She delighted in hearing the fond words coming her husband and children, which caused her to shed tears from time to time. But then, Alice's countenance changed. She appeared to be guarded and defensive, and virtually shut down, emotionally. Alice's family members had to redirect her attention several times by calling her name or tapping her on her shoulder and her leg. Finally, Ralph asked Alice if she was listening to what was being said. She sat quietly for a few moments before bursting into tears. "I think I know what's going on," she cried. "I don't think any of you really know what I have been through before I left my parents' home for college," Alice exclaimed. She was about to drop a bomb on her family that had been hidden for many years.

Alice told her story of being sexual abuse by the hand of a close family friend, and how she refused to tell her parents because this person had been a part of her parents' lives since they were children, and "didn't say anything because it would have caused too much damage." She said she decided to be a teacher "because it was my way to protect children and help them to protect themselves from people like him." To her family's surprise, Alice showed a part of herself that none of them had ever seen before. Alice was animated and emotional. She wanted her family to understand the demeanor they had known all of their lives were because of the abuse she had endured long ago. Alice, as it was discovered, wore a mask to hide her inner turmoil. She was finally ready to tell her story and work through the trauma and emotional scars she had been hiding most of her life.

Alice decided she would seek counsel from a therapist who specialized in sexual trauma. Alice and the therapist met for their first session and quickly established goals for their therapeutic relationship. She stated, "It's about time for me to face my past so I can move on and not feel like a pretender anymore." Alice agreed to tell her story, express how she was able to wear her mask for so long, what was causing her to want to disclose and work through her childhood trauma, and her willingness to risk peace and stability within her family-of-origin. Alice stated, "It's about time that I care for myself. For so many years, I've protected, loved and cared for others'. It's time that I do something for myself." She denied bearing resentment towards the people in her life but admitted that shame had been the basis for her strong, forthcoming attitude and behavior over the years. At the end of their first session, the therapist explained that "these sessions are for you, Alice," and encouraged her to decide on the direction their therapeutic relationship would go. Out of habit, Alice replied, "Whatever you want to talk about is fine with me." The therapist insisted that Alice think of herself "for a change" and he would follow her lead. Alice reluctantly agreed.

When Alice and the therapist met the following week, she sat quietly for the first few moments. The therapist allowed Alice to sit in her silence and reassured her that her silence was normal at that juncture of their therapeutic relationship, and she was free to be herself "in this sacred space." She apologized profusely for her quietness and promised to be more interactive. The therapist asked Alice if she felt a strong need to make him feel comfortable to which she nodded, "yes." She also stated that "pleasing others gives me a sense of satisfaction and meaning in my life." The therapist asked Alice if she felt that pleasing others at all cost really made her life worthwhile or did it make her feel loved and needed. Alice gazed out of a small window without responding momentarily. The therapist sat quietly until Alice gave the subtle cue that she was present. He opened a folder and began to read the following statement:

> We often sacrifice whom we are to make sure that others are happy; we place their need for nurture and growth before our own. The desire to please and be liked becomes so overwhelming at times that we literally lose our sense of self (Wimberly, 1997, p. 66).

Alice sat stunned by what she just heard. Amazed by the therapist's intuitive instinct, Alice said she denied herself through the years and "dared not rock the boat by saying what I really felt." She also disclosed that she felt that pleasing others was expected of her, "like I had no choice." Wimberly (1997) explained this overwhelming sense of duty to others in the following way:

> It is the cognitive belief that our lives will be meaningless and empty if we do not fulfill such expectation. This intimidation propels us into ritualistic, repetitive, self-deprecating behaviors. The fear comes from our view that people would not like us if they saw the real us... Feeling that others would not be interested in her own problems and concerns, minimized them. Denying her vulnerability and the hurt she felt inside, she never let others see her inner pain (p. 67).

Alice stated that she flourished in her role as a "people pleaser" because she was able to avoid facing her self and was able to function in a way that was positive and meaningful to others. She did not like having the spotlight cast upon her, therefore she happily took her place on the sideline, avoiding conflict at all cost, "but when I got tired of something or someone, I spoke my mind. I tried not to be dishonest with people, so I told the truth when I was asked a question."

The therapist and Alice began to process how she managed to fulfill the expectations of pleasing others for so long. She was able to clearly state that "the shame made it possible for me to not want to step out of this role because I was not ready to deal with it. I kept it on the backburner for so long, I never found the appropriate time to face it until now." The therapist helped Alice to understand that she had been living with a form of sexual abuse syndrome most of her life. Alice asked the therapist to give her something concrete to think about before she left this session. She also asked for reading materials for the next session. The therapist agreed and then lifted a sheet of paper and began to read:

> To summarize briefly, in sexual abuse syndromes, intense shame (humiliation) is the predominate affect and is accompanied by fear, distress (sadness, crying), and rage. In the midst of shame, the victim feels to blame—an inevitable result of shame. The violation scene replays itself in consciousness or night terrors, or hover at the periphery of awareness. If instead the scene is banished for awareness, disowned, the self emerges frozen, statuelike (Kaufman, 1996, p. 122).

Alice arrived at the next session chatty and excited. She informed the therapist that she was "ready to spill the beans (confess her shame)." Alice stated she read that "Psychologically, confessing shame or guilt is an attempt to acknowledge that shame has occurred and to relieve it by going to others and telling them about it" (Wimberly, 1999, p. 75; Lewis, 1995, p. 131). Alice added that she intended to do so within the confines of the therapeutic setting before doing so with her family. The therapist assured her that her plan had merit because she would be able to do as one writer espouses:

> ...shame is acknowledged by allowing oneself to be aware of its existence, but one detaches the self from it by placing it outside of the self. This is a way of observing one's shame, in an objective way, apart from the self. Here the externalization enables one to move from being the observed to the observer. Confession is also a way of undoing the original shame scene (Wimberly, 1999, p. 75).

As a result of Alice's confession of long-lived shame to the therapist, they were able to work productively towards her beginning the next chapter of her life. She began to accept her "sunny disposition" in an authentic, not forced, fashion. Alice became excited about her future as a retired teacher and declared, "Once a teacher, always a teacher. It doesn't mean I cannot do other things to help others." Alice was well on her way to achieving self transcendence, which will be discussed later in the section regarding Logotherapy.

Cissy: Striving for Perfection

Cissy is a 27-year-old Caucasian woman. She is a wife, homemaker, and mother of two children—a two-year-old boy and six-month-old girl. She maintains an immaculate household and prepares wonderful meals for her family on a daily basis. From the outside, many would say Cissy takes great pride in caring for her family, and she makes sure things are in place as much as possible. Cissy grew up in a two-parent household, where her father went to work and her mother maintained the home. To her recollection, many of the things her mother had done in her role as a homemaker, she (Cissy) was now doing for her own family today. Cissy reported that her mother used to tell her that she had to learn how to be a "good girl" and uphold her part if she wanted to be a "proper wife" to her husband and "a good mother" to her children; that is, "the conviction that you must be good and gracious at all costs. It is rooted in feelings that you cannot be angry or upset because this will make others uncomfortable. The goal is perfect goodness" (Wimberly, 1997, p. 23).

It appears that Cissy finds joy in entertaining others, as evidenced by her hosting many social events in her home. On Thursday afternoons, she hosts a weekly bridge game with other homemakers in her community. One afternoon, the conversation focused on why they decided to become homemakers. They took turns telling their stories and future aspirations. When it was Cissy's turn, declared she never intended to be "a housewife." To everyone's surprise, Cissy was a Certified Professional Accountant by profession, but stayed home when her son was born. The room remained quiet momentarily before someone asked, "You said that as if you didn't have a choice. So why didn't speak up?" Cissy quietly glared at her friend as if to say, "Don't go there with me." The bridge game continued without much chatter. At the end of the game, Cissy thanked her friends for visiting and said she looked forward to seeing them the following week.

Cissy started to think about the discussion with her friends once she was alone. She contemplated what she would do once her youngest child starts pre-school—whether she will return to the work-force or remain in the home. "After all," she thought, "money isn't an issue because my husband's salary is sufficient to provide for our family's needs." Suddenly, Cissy was distracted by the telephone ringing, which woke her sleeping child up from her nap. She found herself not attending to her child's cries, but was cleaning, wiping, chopping, washing, and cooking profusely. Cissy noticed that she was truly becoming more like her mother—imitating the same cold, listless behavior her mother did when Cissy was a child. She decided to seek the assistance of a counselor because she knew her behavior would eventually cause additional pain, as it did in her family-of-origin.

Remembering the counseling courses she took in college, Cissy recalled a profound statement that one of her former professors made: "An important portion of the counseling process is that the client is willing to participate in the process." Cissy decided to do some "soul searching" to begin seeing herself for who she really was. She also decided to enlist the help of a trusted friend to act as her "emotional sponsor." Cissy's friend agreed to meet with her on a weekly basis for "rap sessions" so that Cissy could become comfortable with expressing some of her feelings. Cissy readily admitted that she functions from the expectations she acquired from her childhood. This is a critical point for Cissy because of her acknowledgement of her own skewed perceptions.

Wimberly (1997) refers to these perceptions of the self as myths. He also spoke of how myths are produced in our lives; and ascribes that some myths cause inner strife and should be reconstructed if the person is willing to do so.

> The nature of myths is to appear fixed and unchangeable. Yet if we understand how myths evolve and see how we participate in their creation, we can discern the possibility of transformation. In the actual process of editing myths, we are surprised to discover that what was once considered closed and permanently fossilized in our being is not only changeable but actually *awaiting* transformation (p. 75).

During one of their rap sessions, Cissy stated she remembers watching how her mother would "do her work" whenever she was stressed out or anxious. "My mom would move around the house feverishly," Cissy recalled, "as if she were in another world." She also remembered her mother saying things like: "I'm in my zone," "I'm busy," and "I've gotta get this done while I'm doing it." In Cissy's mind this meant go away and leave me alone. Cissy openly admitted that she does the same when she feels inadequate, and "I do things around the house really well because I know it's something I'm good at." Kaufman (1996) explained a concept called "the splitting of the self" in the following: "Internal strife waged relentlessly against disowned parts of the self results in an actual *splitting of the self* in two or more partial selves or caricatures of the self" (p. 107). For Cissy, she tends to gain pleasure from the compliments she receives regarding her home and the jokes about her being "anally retentive" about how she must have things done or positioned "right in my home."

By the time that Cissy did enter into her therapeutic relationship with her counselor, she had been working through some of her "surface issues." During the fourth session, Cissy disclosed that one of her greatest sources of anguish is the feeling of powerlessness— "The condition of powerlessness is a psychological phenomenon with profound consequences," Kaufman wrote (p. 47). She also said she saw this in her mother. Cissy shared a moment that left her feeling powerless appeared when the decision was *made* regarding her being a homemaker after her children were born. With a great deal of resentment in her voice and posture, Cissy said she felt that "I did not have a choice in the matter. My husband said his income was enough to sustain our home." Therefore, the discussion ended on that note and she became a homemaker.

Cissy's shame and powerlessness was restored in her adult life. Like her mother, who was married to a passive-aggressive man, Cissy's husband also used shame subtly in order to control her. "Powerlessness experienced anew during adulthood reactivates that earlier governing scene of initial primary helplessness. The adult is then immediately transported back into that original scene and relives it in the present with all its affect reawakened" (Kaufman, 1996, p. 47). Not wanting to "upset my husband," Cissy went along with his wishes because "it was easier to keep the peace." Wimberly (1997) cautioned:

> The myth of powerlessness is the conviction that we have no real power or agency to impact our lives and the lives of others, our environment, and our world. We see other people as having more power and control over our lives than we do. We feel that things happen to us, that we have no real choice or decision. We may feel victimized by others, helpless to respond to what is being done "to us."

> We may become overly vigilant, seeking to identify potential perpetrators before they can abuse us... The danger of perfectionism is that we might see ourselves unrealistically as imperfect or flawed. In our expectation of perfection, there is no possibility for grace-filled self-acceptance. The others whom we envisage as perfect have all the power (p. 19).

In Cissy's mind, she has total control over the upkeep of her household because her husband does not have much say in this regard. Yet she feels trapped in a repeated cycle of acquiescence over her personal power in order to appease someone else. Both, Cissy and her counselor, agreed that a viable step for her to take may be her ability to convey her desire to return to work once her daughter is old enough to attend a daycare. Then, she can focus her energy on something she enjoys and loves—not out of duty.

Danny: Need for Control/Striving for Power

Danny is a 45-year-old, Hispanic American male, who recently began seeing a local Pastoral Counselor because he was no longer happy with his relationships with others lately. He was also at a loss by the reactions he received from others in his life. Danny reported that his attitude towards life and people had not drastically changed, "I've been this way for a long, long time." He described himself as "a take charge kind of person," who steps up when "I see things in need of my touch." The Pastoral Counselor asked Danny to explain his birth order in his family, and how he experienced the decision-making process as a child. Shocked and confused by this inquiry, Danny said he was the youngest of five children, and "Either my parents or older siblings told me what to do, when to do it, and how it was to be done." The Pastoral Counselor suggested that his controlling behavior could be linked to his striving for power within his family-of-origin. Danny asked the Pastoral Counselor to "say more." He was told:

> The need for power is fundamentally a need for inner control over one's own life. A sense of inner control is the felt experience of power. It is a need to be able to influence one's environment, to feel consulted, to have an impact, to feel heard. To experience choice to know power, being able to predict and control what happens. Any life even that

wrenches away that vital sense of inner control activates powerlessness (Kaufman, 1996, p. 79).

Gaining power over others and interpersonal situations, jockeying for position in social groups, and keeping control in relationships are particular manifestations of power scripts. A power script may also grow to dominate the self, eclipsing all other scripts and becoming a way of life. Then power becomes the principle means for maintaining security and enhancing self-esteem. Power becomes the only desired goal (Kaufman, 1996, p. 98).

Danny disclosed that he recalled his first hint of control came when he left home for college. "It was an awesome feeling when people seemed to value my intellect, and they wanted to hear from me," he explained. Danny also shared that "I dreaded going home for the holidays" because he would be in the presence of his family-of-origin. He felt like a child once again being in their presence. Danny revealed that he would usually "sit quietly until someone addresses me directly."

Being that Danny felt comfortable in the learning environment, he decided to pursue a master's degree and live in an apartment within striking distance of his school. He did continue to return home for holidays and breaks. Danny excelled and completed this program a semester earlier than intended. His resilience enabled him to remain in the city he was in—miles away from his family-of-origin. With pride, Danny explained, "Once I finished my education and started working, and I was quickly promoted to management and executive positions." This accounted for his ability to "take charge most of the time." However, the astute Pastoral Counselor sensed there was more to Danny's drive for "being in control." Danny acknowledged that some of his controlling behaviors rewarded him for his feeling inadequate, especially in his family-of-origin's presence, which led to his need to cover his contempt with being controlled as a child. He would "flex" of his intellect muscles as a way for him to hide his shortcomings. Hence, Kaufman (1996) described this striving for perfection in the following manner:

> Perfection scripts organize the self in order to erase every perceived blemish. The self must excel in an ever-widening circle of activities, while nothing done is ever seen as good

enough. Perfecting the self comprises a set of rules for responding to magnified scenes of shame. In predicting and controlling shame scenes, perfectionism is an attempt to compensate for feeling inherently defective, never quite good enough as a person. Hence, the perception that nothing done is ever good enough—it could always have been better. The inevitable result is that one is plunged back into shame. Perfection scripts are therefore both self-limiting and self-validating (p. 97).

Danny began to realize that his controlling behaviors were becoming something that others were no longer willing to tolerate. He saw the need to reconfigure his life and how he related to others around him. "I get it," he excitedly announced, "people like me for who I am, not my obnoxious, pretentious behavior. That makes it hard for them to be around me." It was evident that Danny was ready to begin his new journey.

Isn't It A Shame?

When shame is allowed to grow and fester, as with many other human characteristics, it can have paralyzing affects on a person's development. Although shame may be the way a person can recognize that their actions may be harmful physically, psychologically, and emotionally to themselves and/or others, if left unchecked, it can also cause a person to feel crippled by their own thoughts and feelings. In many ways, people do not want to feel restricted or limited. Generally, people want to be free to live and move without embarrassment and humiliation. Unchecked toxic shame hinders these ambitions by leaving a person feeling stuck in their own negative views of themselves and/or other people's ill-conceived perceptions of them. Shame is seen both externally and internally as it is experienced by the individual. Whether the person experienced physical, sexual, emotional abuse or not, shame can also come from growing up in an environment where there was alcoholism, infidelity, mental illness or defect, and so on. In order to break the cycle of shaming or shame-filled behaviors, one must face their own "demons" and call them what they are—stifling, life robbing, hindering spirits.

Based on human instinct, people seek to protect themselves as they sense danger. Psychologically, emotionally and physically, the body reacts to threats, which causes automatic responses to occur. Kaufman (1996) reported the following:

> The shame response of hanging the head or lowering the eyes is a response that causes an immediate reduction of facial visibility, which is why we have historically referred to shame in terms of *loss of face*... Hanging one's head in shame deeply mortifies the spirit, whether as individuals, families, or nations. Loss of face itself is further cause for shame. Inevitably, **there is shame about shame** (p. 19, emphasis mine).

In his observation of Darwin's treatment of facial expression in regard to shame, Lewis (1995) added:

> Darwin said that when one is ashamed the head is averted or bent down with the eyes wavering or turned away (what is now referred to as gaze avert). Darwin noted that facial blushing is a manifestation of shame, and he also pointed out that the reddening of the skin, the bringing of blood vessels to the surface, takes place not only in the facial region but all over the body... ...because the face is the seat of one's identity, and one wishes to conceal oneself during shame, the face becomes the focus of the shame. By logical extension, the degree to which other parts of the body become the focus might influence the degree to which they also would blush (pp. 22, 23).

People also respond to shame with inward emotional expressions. Kaufman (1996) called these expressions defending scripts. He stated, "Examining the individual's developing rules for responding to, predicting, controlling, and interpreting a magnified set of shame scenes will illuminate the particular strategies of defense that develop to protect the self against further encounters with shame" (p. 97). Both Lewis (1995) and Kaufman (1996) discussed rage, contempt, and the transference of blame, internal withdrawal, humor, and denial as methods that the individuals use to protect themselves from threats of potential harm. Each of the aforementioned behaviors can appear in a variety of experiences and settings. Kaufman spoke of rage in the following terms: "Whether in the form of generalized hostility, fomenting bitterness, chronic hatred, or explosive eruptions, rage protects the self against exposure" (p. 96). In other words, people who appear to be angry, mad or mean may be the very ones who seek to guard themselves from situations where their shame might be uncovered. Lewis expounded on the affects of long-term shame and rage in the ensuing fashion:

> People who are continuously shamed by others can develop rage. This rage may be expressed toward those causing them shame or displayed to other for a variety of reasons: the other may be too powerful, the other may pose a physical threat, the other may be someone for whom the shamed person feels strong positive emotions, and therefore with whom rage would be incompatible with other feelings, etc. In addition, the rage may be deflected because the other is needed (p. 151).

The person whom seems to be an angry person may not have always been that way. They may have developed this behavior or demeanor as a way of shielding themselves based on their experiences of being shamed in the past— "...rage organizes and interprets new experiences in order to control magnified scenes of shame, and to predict and respond to future ones" (Kaufman, 1996, p. 97).

Contempt can be similar to rage in that it can appear to be more subtle in its manifestations. Kaufman's (1996) treatment of contempt as it relates to shame was powerfully demonstrated when he wrote:

> A blend of dissmell and anger, contempt distances the self from others while elevating the self above others. To the degree that others are looked down upon, found lacking or seen as lesser or inferior beings, a once wounded self becomes more securely insulated against further shame. Contempt is the source of conceit, arrogance and superiority, of judgmental, fault-finding or condescending attitudes toward others. Contempt scripts reinterpret new experiences in order to avoid or escape from shame (p. 97).

Shifting or placing the blame on other people, environments and/or circumstance are also manifestations of shame. Lewis (1995) declared, "People violate standards, rules, and goals but often do not attribute the failure to themselves. Instead, they may explain their failure in terms of chance or the actions of others" (p. 68). For example, Johnny was caught with his hand in the cookie jar by his mother. His response should be, "You caught me with my hand in the cookie jar." But he might go as far to say his mother was seeing things or she should have put them somewhere else. "Blaming focuses attention upon who can be found responsible for any mishap or misdeed that occurs," Kaufman explained, "Blaming is a strategy that recruits the effect of anger, but directs it in an accusatory, fault-finding manner" (p. 98). In other words, blaming others is an attempt to get one's self "off the hook," so to speak.

Many times, a person who have experienced repeated shame might pull away from others and social settings and withdraw into themselves. "Withdrawing deeper inside the self is another strategic alternative," Kaufman (1996, p. 99) asserted. The shamed person might find that keeping away from people, places and environments may be the only way to protect their self and to avoid situations where they might be shamed once again. Kaufman continued on to clarify the outward effects of internal withdrawal when he wrote:

> This [withdrawal] script reduces exposure and avoids further shame by withdrawing the self deeper inside, allowing escape from the torment of shame. The agony of exposure is thereby reduced, and the loss of the possibility of reunion is also neutralized. The self in effect hides from shame by hiding deeper inside. Only a superficial social mask remains, visible, knowable by others. The real self—the needing, feeling, imagining self—has shut itself in. In response, the individual increasingly becomes a shut-in personality (p. 99).

Interestingly, humor and/or laughter can serve as a light-hearted shield for a shamed person. Lewis (1995) wrote, "Laughter also is a mechanism by which the acknowledged shame can be reduced or eliminated" (p. 130). It is a way a person can shake off the negative feelings that can surface as a result of a shame-filled experience. Lewis continued on to say,

> ...laughing at one's self serves to distance one's self from the emotional experience... Because laughter is such a powerful stimulus, it allows us to focus on another emotion, and thereby enables us to defocus the shame. ...laughter, especially laughter around one's transgression

as it occurs in a social context, provides the opportunity for the transgressing person to join others in viewing the self. In this way, the self metaphorically moves from the site of the shame to the site of observing the shame with the other (p. 130).

Kaufman (1996) added that "Humor attenuates [satisfy, calm, soothe, or ease] the self-consciousness and exposure inherent in the shame. The self's momentary estrangement—feeling strange, ill-at-ease, discomfort, or alienation—is alleviated by the shared enjoyment experienced through humor" (p. 99). Many times, we see people making jokes out of events or actions that they were a part of and laugh just as hard as the next person. This may be their way of getting through the humiliation unscathed.

Finally, the discussions of denial proved to be revealing in its content. Kaufman (1996) wrote, "Denial functions just like other scripts, guarding the boundary between self and their environment. Denial scripts attempt to exclude shame from awareness by denying its perception, or by denying the perception of anything that might arouse shame" (p. 100). In a way, a shamed person will act as if the situation or their feelings do not exist by saying it did not happen or it is not occurring. Lewis (1995) added that "Denial can act to prevent shame from occurring. Denial is not the same as forgetting [it happened]" (p. 129). In other words, the shamed person may simply resort to not acknowledging that an infraction took place. They avoid accepting the action or feeling as their own. Lewis continued on to say,

> This ideation (denial) represents an attempt to move the self away from the shame through denial that anything bad has occurred.... But it may be true that denial sometimes operates prior to the shame experience, preventing it from occurring, as well as after the shame experience, as a way of bypassing the feeling... ...we can use denial to prevent the internal attribution of blame. If a person prevents such attribution, then no shame will occur..." (p. 129).

In the religious realm, denial can be seen in what is called religiosity. The concept of religiosity is defined as "An excessive or affected religious zeal. It connotes an outward display of actions without a correspondingly genuine valuing of religion" (McKim, 1996, p. 236). This behavior may be used as a shield from shame-filled situations. In my Pastoral Counseling experience, I have had an opportunity to witness this type of behavior on several occasions. Rather than dealing with the reality of an experience, the person would refer to either a biblical reference or the use of an extreme amount of piety (goodness) to avoid dealing with what's going on around them. They avoid direct questions, curtail topics by rambling on about religious or biblical items, and/or refuse to answer all together by referring to a higher being in control or instructing their incompliance. Religiosity in of itself is yet another defense mechanism that protects the self from further or future shame.

<u>It Gets in the Way</u>

As previously mentioned, if shame is nurtured in a suitable environment, it can grow and spread with deadly consequences likened to cancer. One of the most destructive yet effective ways in which shame flourishes is through secrets and/or "discreetness," where a person or a group of persons seeks to hide incidents they deem shameful. Bradshaw (1996) spoke of keeping secrets in the following way: "The ability to keep things secret is an essential power that all human beings possess in order to protect themselves" (p. 5). When secrets are created to protect one's self or others in unhealthy ways, they tend to stifle those who may be seen as the "cause" and/or the victim—I use victim because the secret tends to trap them in a cycle of trying to keep the secret hidden. Allender (1990), spoke of the fear we have of our secret shame being seen in light of others, even God:

> Shame is a dreaded, deep-seated, long-held terror come: what we have feared has actually come about. We've been found out. The *dark secret*—and there many in every life—that may involve a past sexual indiscretion, thought or behavior, a past disloyalty, a failure of conscience, a violent act, a cruel outburst, or personal failure is known. All out elaborate defenses, disguises, and personality traits are held in bondage to the goal of not being known because to be known is to be caught. ...Therefore, to avoid the awkwardness of other peoples' discomfort, the patronizing support of those who do not understand the internal damage, and worse, the subtle implication that it was their fault, it seems better to hide behind the cloak of denial (p. 63, emphasis mine).

All too often people learn ways to hide the shame that takes place in their home with their family members. Branson and Silva (2007), while discussing domestic violence, conveyed a powerful description of how family members work together to maintain their public image as they keep their secrets:

> From all outward appearances, both families appear to be loving parents who provide a healthy home environment for their children. They are well respected in their neighborhood, at work, and at church. Yet behind the walls of one of these homes a well-kept secret hide—a secret that may not be obvious to their neighbor, friend, or family, and perhaps not even their pastor. Each member of the family guards the secret, sometimes for decades, as if telling anyone would detonate a hidden explosive that would destroy them all. ...They live on an emotional rollercoaster, never knowing whether to expect fun and games or rage and destruction—never knowing whether they are going to awaken a gentle giant or an angry ogre (pp. 11, 12).

The point of this quote is to say, shame-based secrets, and the behaviors that accompany them, can be poisonous for all involved in keeping them hidden. Bradshaw (1990), who wrote extensively about family secrets and shame, discussed the ways in which adults try to "protect" their children by not disclosing needed information, such as tragic events, illness, death, divorce, etc. He said, "When such traumatic events are denied and made into dark secrets, a family's loyalty to the secret may appear in subsequent generations as reclusiveness, morbid fear, obsession with death, bizarre and explainable death-defying crazy behavior, and suicide attempts on an anniversary or at the same age as the first death" (p. 29). Behaviors and/or rationales that are conveyed and kept within the family are ultimately construed as lies when discovered, especially those truth-filled messages that are withheld.

It is important to know that there is a distinct difference between privacy and secrecy. Privacy, in my opinion, is the right to withhold pertinent personal information from others, such as one's social security number; on the other hand, secrecy tends to cover something up. Bradshaw (1990) also made this distinction when he spoke of toxic shame: "When our natural shame, which guards our privacy and the unique dignity of our self is violated, we take on a false, pretend self that is shameless" (p. 29). This type of behavior may become a bottomless pit, so to speak, depending on the individual. Bradshaw continued on to distinguish two categories of shamelessness:

> We act shameless by attempting to transcend our limits as human beings, we try to be *more than human*—we act perfect (we never make mistakes), we act needless (we need no help from anyone), we act righteous (we are caved and others are not), we act authoritarian (we have the right to violate others' space), we act patronizing (we know it all). At the other extreme we can act shameless by acting *less than human*. We let others violate us or we violate ourselves. We become shameful failures, victims, addict—the dregs of society. We are so hopeless, we lose all sense of limits. We believe that everything about us is flawed and defective (p. 29, emphasis mine).

This perspective is crucial to our understanding of shame-filled behaviors. What appears on the surface is not always what it really is deep inside. The behavior can be linked to shame or learned shame-based behaviors. Secrets tend to eat away at one's conscious, at one's soul. Within a family unit, whether it is the immediate or extended family, exposed secrets are like airing dirty laundry for all to see and smell. In order to keep these things from surfacing, silence and/or conspiracies are spun to keep information withheld and out of sight. Bradshaw (1990) spoke of toxic shame and dark secrets in the following manner:

> Toxic shame forces us to literally lose face and then to try and save face. In order to save face, we go into hiding and isolation. We seek ways to always be in control. We guard lest we ever be caught off guard. We live covering up our pain. This requires an arsenal of secrets. We have secrets to cover secrets, lies to cover other lies. Toxic shame affects not just our *doing* but our very *being*. Deep down we feel like something is very wrong with us. Toxic shame demands that I wear a mask, put on a disguise, develop a false self. If I were to let you see me as I really am, you would see that I am flawed and defective and reject me. I must therefore remain silent (p. 30, emphasis mine).

No Shame in the Game

This quotation helps us in our understanding of how shame and dark secrets diminish our sense of self. It *forces* us to create layers of fake versions of our selves—a public self, a familial self, a social self, etc. The danger of having multi-layered selves is the authentic self can be lost along the way.

I had a conversation with a woman who shared a long-hidden secret with me. This admission seemed to have come "out of nowhere," but as she warned: "It's time I say something because I'm tired of this [explicative]!" In my heart and mind, I was thinking, "Oh God, help me." I also prayed that I was not being pulled into an ongoing circle of secret holders. As it turned out, this woman said, "I'm going to confront the people who were involved." This young woman assured me that she would make sure she would maintain her safety—physically and mentally. She had planned "not to share the same space with the other parties." This woman garnered strength by taking a deep, silent breath. "I'm an incest survivor!" she said. She went on to say her plan was to write a letter to her uncle and father, detailing how the abuse robbed her of her self "before I had the chance to discover who I am." She also indicated that she intended to write and send a letter to her mother as well because, "She did not protect me and turned the other cheek when she knew what was going on." This brave woman was willing to risk alienating herself from her family in order to free herself from a vicious cycle of shame-based dark secrets.

It is my hope that as we proceed that you, the reader, will come to a deeper understanding of the workings of shame, and be willing and able to acknowledge and address your inner struggles with it. As Allender (2008) astutely wrote: "Contempt is condemnation, an attack against the perceived cause of the shame. The attack [by the opposing enemy, Satan] is laced with hatred, venom, and icy cruelty, though it can be as insidious as a warm smile and gentle rebuke" (pp. 74 – 75). One of the most destructive wiles the enemy uses is our emotions, especially when they are impaired. God made us to be wholly complex, even in what seems to be flaws. Our goal is to grab hold of them, understand them, check them, and use them to minister to others through our testimonies. Therefore, we need to be able to acknowledge them and press forward in our journeys through life.

Dr. Kasim Ali Sidney Jones

No Shame in the Game

Part Two:
The Price Paid for Shame

"Nevertheless, there will be no more gloom for those who were in distress. In the past he humbled the land of Zebulun and the land of Naphtali, but in the future he will honor Galilee of the Gentiles, by the way of the along the Jordan.... For to us a child is born, to us a son is given, and the government will be on his shoulders. And he will be called Wonderful Counselor, Mighty God, Everlasting Father, Prince of Peace. Of the increase of his government and peace there will be no end. He will reign on David's throne and over his kingdom, establishing and upholding it with justice and righteousness from that time on and forever. The zeal of the LORD Almighty will accomplish this."

Isaiah 9: 1, 6 – 7 (*New International Version*)

"In the beginning was the Word (logos), and the Word (logos) was with God, and the Word (logos) was God. He was with God in the beginning. Through him all things were made; without him nothing was made that has been made. In him was life, and that life was the light of men. The light shines in the darkness, but the darkness has not understood it... He was in the world, and though the world was made through him, the world did not recognize him. He came to that which was his own did not receive him. Yet to all who received him, to those who believed in his name, he gave the right to become children of God...."

John 1: 1 – 5, 10 - 12 (*New International Version*)

The Wonderful Counselor

Who is this Wonderful Counselor? someone might ask. The Wonderful Counselor is Jesus the Christ, our Lord and our Savior. This section was the most exciting yet challenging for me because of who I am in Christ—a counselor/clinician, a Youth Pastor, and simply a child of God. My initial temptation was to compose this portion in a sermonic fashion. Praise God for prayer and obedience! I was able to settle down, do the research and the reading in order to do justice to it. A word that came to me from my seminary days was EXEGESIS (and I shiver)! I was reminded that I needed to keep this section in line with this project's intended themes: shame and Logotherapy. Therefore, using the Gospel According to St. John, I set out to outline Jesus' interaction with three people within his community: Nicodemus, the Samaritan woman at the well, and the lame man at the pool of Bethesda. These exchanges will show how Jesus led these people to meaning in their lives, and therefore, delivered them.

I chose to use the Gospel According to St. John because the author described the life and ministry of Jesus from an individual/communal perspective. It is in this account that we find Jesus interacting with individuals and the community on an intimate level. And the Gospel According to St. John Jesus portrayed as the logos, the Word within Holy Trinity. The three characters presented below, as you will discover, all struggled with some form of shame to which Jesus delivered them from.

The Lowest of Highs: Nicodemus

In John 3: 1 – 21, we find Jesus interacting with Nicodemus, a Pharisee and a member of the Sanhedrin, "a court of seventy members and was the supreme court of the Jews" (Barclay, 1975, p. 123). Being a Pharisee, Nicodemus was considered one of "the best people in the whole country," according to Barclay (1975, p. 120). He went on further to describe Pharisees in deeper details:

> ...they were what were known as a *chaburah*, brotherhood. They entered into this brotherhood by taking a pledge in front of three witnesses that they would spend all their

lives observing every detail of the scribal law... ...it was the *Pharisees* who dedicated their lives to keeping them. Obviously, however misguided a man might be, he must be desperately in earnest if he proposed to undertake obedience to every one of the thousands of rules. That is precisely what the Pharisees did. The name *Pharisee* means *the Separate One*; and the Pharisees were those who had separated themselves from all ordinary life in order to keep every detail of the law of the scribe. ...and it is astonishing that a man who regarded goodness in that light and who had given himself to that kind of life in the conviction that he was pleasing God should wish to talk to Jesus at all (pp. 120, 122 – 123).

It is believed Nicodemus was well off because "When Jesus died Nicodemus brought for his body 'a mixture of myrrh and aloes about a hundred pound weight' (John 19: 39), and only a wealthy man could have brought that" (Barclay, 1975, p. 120). Many scholars and historians also believe Nicodemus came from a wealthy family that made great contributions in history. If this is true, Nicodemus' pedigree may have prompted a certain amount of shame in his life because when he and Jesus talked about spiritual matters, Nicodemus found himself confused by what Jesus taught. When we think about Ezra's situation, he was confounded by the fact that he was reared in a home environment where many things were hidden, while other social messages were promoted. Once Ezra began to realize there was a huge contradiction in what he was taught and by what he was experiencing, his life began to take complicated turns. This seemed to be the case for Nicodemus as well.

What is interesting about Nicodemus' contact with Jesus is that it occurred at night. Being a leader of the Jews, we could only imagine why Nicodemus aired on the side of caution by coming to Jesus in the first place, let alone at night. Moloney (1998) explained this encounter as "The movement of Nicodemus, a leader of 'the Jews,' toward Jesus, coming from the darkness of the night into the light, is a significant movement toward believing, receiving the one sent to make God known" (p. 91). In essence, Nicodemus was taking a great risk in meeting with Jesus. "Nicodemus was a puzzled man, a man with many hours and yet with something lack in his life. He came to Jesus for a talk so that somehow in the darkness of the night he might find light" (Barclay, 1975, p. 124). Nicodemus wanted to be freed through enlightenment.

It is apparent that Nicodemus held Jesus in high regards because in John 3: 2b he said, "Rabbi, we know that you are a teacher come from God; for no one can do these signs that you do, unless God is with you." Jesus, in his answer, knew who Nicodemus was and his role in the community. Nicodemus was an expert of Jewish law and committed himself to living such a life in accordance with those laws; however, those laws were not enough to satisfy what was missing from his life. This is evidenced by Nicodemus calling Jesus rabbi, which is a sign of high esteem. Moloney (1998) asserted that "Nicodemus joins these first, fragile believers in Jesus, and goes further in accepting that he is a teacher from God and the signs he does are an indication that God is with him, a dignity reserved for the great figures of Israel" (p. 91).

As Nicodemus and Jesus began to engage in a discussion of being born again or radically changed, Nicodemus misunderstood what was said to him. This is shown by Nicodemus asking, '"How can a person be born after having grown old? Can one enter a second time into his mother's womb and be born?"' (v. 4). Being well steeped in the Jewish law, which also meant he was an expert in the Books of the Law (the first five books of the Old Testament, the Pentateuch), the concept of being "born again" was a great departure from Nicodemus' understanding of spiritual matters. For Jesus, being "born again" meant, "the important thing was such change in a man's inner life that it could only be described as a new birth" (Barclay 1975, p. 124).

Within this encounter, Nicodemus demonstrated signs of a person who felt trapped in tradition and longed for a greater understanding of what Jesus taught. Barclay (1975) said:

> But there is more to Nicodemus' answer than that. In his heart there was a great unsatisfied longing. It is as if he said with infinite, wishful yearning: 'You talk about being born anew; you talk about this radical, fundamental change which is so necessary. I know that it is *necessary*; but in my experience it is *impossible*. There is nothing I would like more; but you might as well tell me, a full grown

man, to enter into my mother's womb and be born all over again.' It is not the *desirability* of this change that Nicodemus questioned; that he knew only too well; it is the *possibility* (p. 125).

If you recall, a part of the definition of shame deals with the perception of others or the appearance of something amiss. For Nicodemus, he feared his belief in Jesus being discovered by the other members of the Jewish community; his status could have been jeopardized had he been seen conversing with Jesus. After all Jesus' teachings centered around people needing to change the way they held up the status quo in the way they lived and worshiped God— "Nicodemus is up against the eternal problem, the problem of the man who wants to be changed and who cannot change himself" (Barclay, 1975, 125).

He Who Knows: the Samaritan Woman at the Well

John 4: 6 – 30; 39 – 42 tells the story of Jesus interacting with a Samaritan woman at a well called Jacob's well (v. 6). This encounter occurred in a city called Sychar (v. 5). Moloney (1998) stated that "On two accounts Jesus should not speak to her: she is a woman and she is a Samaritan" (pp. 116 – 117). Yet Jesus engages her anyhow by saying, "Give me a drink" (v. 7). To Jesus, it did not matter what her ethnic background was. He wanted a drink and she was thirsty for liberation from her past. "I think that the Samaritan woman must have unburdened her soul to this stranger. How else could Jesus known of her tangled domestic affair? For one of the very few times in her life she had found one with kindness in his eyes instead of critical superiority; and she opened her heart" (Barclay, 1975, p. 148). This woman's past made her weary and skeptical of others but with Jesus, she felt comfortable. Even though he was a Jew and she a Samaritan, there was something different about Jesus' character to her.

Within this encounter, Jesus "shows us the reality of his humanity," because he "was weary with the journey, and he sat by the side of the well exhausted" (Barclay, 1975, pp. 148 – 149). Jesus took the time to engage this woman without considering the scandal this encounter could have sparked. Barclay (1975) asserted the following:

It shows us the warmth of his sympathy. From an ordinary

religious leader, from one of the orthodox church leaders of the day the Samaritan woman would have fled in embarrassment. She would have avoided such one. If by any unlikely chance he had spoken to her she would have met him with an ashamed and even a hostile silence. But it seemed the most natural thing in the world to talk to Jesus. She had at last met someone who was not a critic but a friend, one who did not condemn but who understood (p. 149).

This woman knew of her past, the traditions of the Jewish leaders, and the possible penalties she could have accrued if she had been caught talking with Jesus. However, Jesus' intent was to penetrate social walls that the two groups had built over the years— "for Jews had nothing in common with Samaritans" (John 4: 9b). Barclay (1975) further explained this barrier between the Jews and the Samaritans in this manner:

The quarrel between the Jews and the Samaritans was an old, old story. Away back about 720 B. C. the Assyrians had invaded the northern kingdom of Samaria and had captured and subjugated it. ...Almost inevitably they (Samaritans) began to inter-marry with the incoming foreigners; and thereby they committed with the Jew was an unforgiveable crime. They lost their racial purity (p. 149).

Jesus intended to give this woman something she needed, "living water" (v. 10) from "a spring of water welling up to eternal life" (v. 14b). When Jesus spoke of a water that would quench one's thirst, the woman's response was, "You don't have a bucket and where is this living water?" (vv. 11 – 12). Moloney (1998) asserted that "There is a battle of wills in this first part of the discussion. Jesus' command arouses an arrogant response from the woman (vv. 7 – 9) but he wrests back the authority, speaking of a gift (vv. 10 – 14) that the woman completely misunderstands (v. 15)" (p. 115). Steeped in the longstanding rift between Jews and Samaritans, she mistook Jesus' words to be physical in their content. "She was jesting with a kind of humouring contempt about eternal things. ...In every man [person] there is this nameless unsatisfied longing; this vague discontent; this something lacking; this frustration" (p. 155). Ironically, this woman's dialogue is similar to that of Nicodemus' talk with Jesus.

Barclay (1975) stated that "We have to note that this conversation with the Samaritan woman follows exactly the same pattern as the conversation with Nicodemus" (p. 152). This may be indicative of human nature, when we do not understand something new we will either question it with a hint of skepticism, take it the wrong way, or reject it flat out. Barclay goes on to say:

> Jesus makes a statement. The statement is taken in the wrong sense. Jesus remakes the statement in an even more vivid way. It is still misunderstood; and then compels the person with whom he is speaking to discover and to face the truth for [himself or] herself. That was Jesus' usual way of teaching; and it was a most effective way.... (p. 152).

The Samaritan woman also reverted to her traditional teachings. However, when she "...raises the question about other figures, like Jacob, and inquired whether the well Jesus referred to as the 'spring of life'" (v. 10). It also shows that her traditional views were more important than the other wells and figures. This may have been this woman's way of trying to divert Jesus' attention away from her people's history and her own past. A simple way of saying this is, this woman attempted to use the evasive skills she probably learned from being around her family and community; likened to Gideon when the angel of the Lord approached him in Judges 6. Gideon's response to the angel, after being called a "mighty warrior," was: "But sir, how can I deliver Israel? My clan is the weakest in Manasseh, and I am the least in my family" (Judges 6: 15, *NRSV*). Because of what Gideon had been told about his family and what he believed about himself, he was not able to see what God was telling him about himself immediately—you are the mighty warrior who will save Israel. This woman may have felt the same about herself and her people.

Jesus was setting the stage to delve into the woman's past transgressions, which caused her to feel like an outcast, physically, emotionally and spiritually. "Suddenly and stabbingly Jesus brought her to her senses. The time for verbal by-play was past; the time for jesting was over" (Barclay, 1975, p. 156). Similar to the way that we incorporate mental and verbal defense mechanisms when someone does not know they scratched the surface of something we are trying to hide, Jesus allowed this woman to do the same. In verse 16, Jesus commanded: "go, call your husband and come back" (*NIV*). Here is where the focus of the exchange shifts.

When Jesus directed the Samaritan woman to go get her husband, he did so to help her concentrate on the inner turmoil she was entrenched in. This woman had to be flabbergasted by this request because the Scriptures said she replied, "I have no husband" (v. 17). Moloney (1998) stated:

> The woman's reply, that she has no husband (v. 17), is to be regarded as an accurate reflection of her current situation. She regards herself as not married to the man with whom she is currently living. Jesus compliments her for telling the truth: "You say well 'I have no husband' (v. 17b). ...She has lived an irregular married life and is currently in a sinful situation, but point of v. 18 is not to lay bare her sinfulness. The focus is on Jesus' power to know the secrets of her intimate life. ...His claim to give living water was beyond her grasp, but a person who tells her about the secrets of her life commands her attention. *No deep spiritual insight is present in her coming to the conviction that this man must have prophetic qualities.* However, there is a marked progression from her addressing his as "a Jew" (v. 9) and "sir" (vv. 11, 15, 19a). Her suggestion that Jesus might be a Jewish prophet raises a further issue, which broaches, but that Jesus transcends (vv. 20 – 26) (p. 127, emphasis mine).

In many ways, we have to face our stuff in a similar manner as this woman did and accept it somehow. "She was suddenly compelled to face herself and the looseness and immorality and total inadequacy of her life," Barclay (1975 p. 156) said. Maybe our situation is not the same as this woman's but we must face our own stuff. Barclay goes on further to offer the following explanation:

> There are two revelations in Christianity: the revelation of God and the revelation of ourselves. No man [or woman] sees himself [or herself] until he [or she] sees himself [themselves] in the presence of Christ; and then he [or she] is appalled at the sight. There is another way of putting it— Christianity begins with a sense of sin. It begins with the

sudden realization that life as we are living it will not do. We awake to ourselves and we awake to our need of God (pp. 156 – 157).

How awesome is this explanation! That may very well be the most challenging realization we could arrive at in our lives. Someone once said righteousness is the hard part, but sin... That's easy. Seeing ourselves as we are shockingly painful. We sometimes convince ourselves that we are "just fine," and not in need of improvement. But we must realize that we need God!

Score the Final Point: The Lame Man

The story of the lame man found in John 5, in many ways, reflects our limitations and how they become a part of lives and functioning. In John 5, the story says Jesus was on his way to Jerusalem for the Feast of the Jews when he encounters a man who had been crippled for thirty-eight years near a pool called Bethesda. Jesus asked him, "Do you want to get well?" (vv. 1 – 6, NIV). Keep in mind that this person had been unable to do certain things for himself for a long time and grew accustomed to being in this condition as seen in his response to Jesus: "Sir I have no one to help me..." (v. 7). This man had to get to a place where he was tired of being dependent upon others because Jesus told him to "Get up! Pick up your mat and walk" (v. 8). Verse 9 says, "At once the man was cured; he picked up his mat and walked." The lame man had to come to a point where he had to want to be healed, where he wanted to do something for himself, and he wanted to be out of the condition he had been in for all of those years. Barclay (1975) made a powerful point when he said:

> The power of God never dispenses with the effort of man. Nothing is truer than that we must realize our own helplessness; but in a very real sense it is true that miracles happen when our will and God's power co-operate to make them possible. ...The man might well have said with a kind of injured resentment that for thirty-eight years his bed been carrying him and there was not much sense in telling him to carry it. But he made the effort along with Christ—and the thing was done (p. 180).

It's interesting how certain human behaviors do not change over time. At times, we tend to linger on in our stifling conditions and complain at the same time— "I'm tired of...." We seek comfort and advice from others, and then, return to the same place we just left. It is not for me to name conditions at this time, but you know your situation. Jesus has been pointing us in the direction we should travel in order to be free. We get excited in knowing that Jesus is rooting for us, and then, we do a complete 360 degree and end up where we started. Case and point is the crab in the barrel mentality, where the people around us do not want to see us be delivered from the things that hold us back. We continue to allow them to be in our lives and wonder why we cannot seem to move on. Clearly stated, they do not want us to turn away from our destructive ways. Barclay (1975) painted a vivid picture of this type of scene when he wrote:

> A man had been healed from a disease which, humanly speaking, was incurable. We might expect this to be an occasion of universal joy and thanksgiving; but some met the whole business with bleak and black looks. The man who had been healed was walking through the street carrying his bed; the orthodox Jews *stopped* him and *reminded* him that he was breaking the law by carrying a burden on the Sabbath day (p. 181, emphasis mine).

Think back to the definition of shame for a moment. Notice that I placed emphasis on two words in the quotation above—stopped and reminded. Today, we call people who want to hold us back, block our paths, or envy what we are doing or where we are going, haters. Their job is to stop us by reminding us that we were born and raised in the hood, we were broke two years ago, and so on. But Jesus says YOU ARE FREE! Don't you remember that I paid the price when I died for you? Complacency is a stronghold of the enemy that can only be broken with the help of the Lord. Your focus cannot be fixed on your past. After all, Jesus taught his disciples, after healing the demon possessed boy in Matthew 17: 14 - 23, but this kind [of condition] does not go out except by prayer and fasting..." (Matthew 17: 21, AMB; this verse is not included in many translations). That's what Jesus says to us when we find ourselves caught in the vicious cycle of living in bondage.

No Shame in the Game

Part Three:
Living with Significance

"The thief's purpose is to steal and kill and destroy. My purpose is to give life in all its fullness."

John 10: 10 (*New Living Translation*)

"So make every effort to apply the benefits of these promises to your life. Then your faith will produce a life of moral excellence. A life of moral excellence leads to knowing God better. Knowing Gods leads to self-control. Self-control leads to patient endurance, and patient endurance leads to godliness. Godliness leads to love for other Christians, and finally you will grow to have genuine love for everyone. The more you grow like this, the more you will become productive and useful in your knowledge of our Lord Jesus Christ. But those who fail to develop these virtues are blind or, at least, very shortsighted. They have already forgotten that God has cleansed them from their old life of sin"

2 Peter 1: 5 – 11 (*New Living Translation*)

What Do You Mean?

Seeing how Jesus ministered to the social outcasts, the sick, the spiritually deprived, and the poor, we have a better understanding as to how many different types of ministries developed over the 2,000 years since Jesus' ascension. I am a firm believer in the psalmist's words: "The earth is the LORD's, and everything in it, the world, and all who live in it..." (Psalm 24:1, *NIV*). God made all things for the glory of God's self, and that includes all kinds of methods of healing and wholeness. We are blessed with a variety of therapeutic methods, treatments, medicines, and natural resources to help us live better lives. This is also true of Frankl's Logotherapy.

I was introduced to Logotherapy while studying at the Interdenominational Theological Center (the ITC), and it was the primary theory of my doctoral dissertation. I became galvanized by how Frankl was able to bring together a crucial aspect of Jesus' ministry of reaching and teaching portions of the population in need of healing into a working theory. Although Frankl did not initially set out to center this concept on the works of Jesus, he did acknowledge that Logotherapy could be beneficial in the Christian setting later in his life. In this theory, Frankl designed a method to help us to see, live and function as God intended—living and serving beyond our selfish motives in order to share with others. What is most intriguing about this therapeutic concept is that it helps people to tap into their God-given purpose (meaning), especially during challenging times in their lives. However, before I discuss Logotherapy further, allow me to introduce the person that formulated it, Viktor E. Frankl.

Viktor Emil Frankl was born on March 26, 1905 in Vienna. He was reared in a middle-class family, and "From his childhood he sensed a depth to life that went beyond material comfort" (Fabry, 1987, p. 7). According to Joseph B. Fabry, one of Frankl's closest friends and students, Frankl had been precociously curious since he was a child and often searched for meaning and asked many questions that may have seemed beyond his age. Fabry wrote of a story of when Frankl was fourteen years old. He stunned his teacher and other students when he asked: "If that is so, then what meaning does life have?" in response to his teacher's statement that "life in the last analysis was nothing but a process of combustion" (pp. 7 - 8). Frankl corresponded with Sigmund Freud while in high school, following the suicidal death of another student. After graduating from high school, Frankl went on to earn doctorate degrees in medicine and in philosophy from the University of Vienna. "As a medical student Frankl became a member of the inner circle of Alfred Adler, the founder of individual psychology," Fabry explained, "but [he] gradually moved away from the orthodox Adlerian view, which led to Frankl's eventual exclusion from the Adlerian Society in Vienna" (p. 8). Frankl's thoughts and opinions caused him to split from the Adlerian school of thought. He felt that the contemporary theories of the day were limited and "what was needed was to understand the human being in his or her totality" (Graber, 2004, p. 17).

Once Frankl completed medical school in 1930, he established a counseling center for teens in distress. It was "Here the fundamental formulations of Logotherapy took shape," Fabry (1987) asserted. He also said of Frankl's Logotherapy:

> ...all reality has meaning (logos) and that life never ceases to have meaning for anyone; that meaning is very specific and changes from person to person and for unique and each life contains a series of unique demands that have to be discovered and responded to, that the response to these provides meaning; and that happiness, contentment, peace of mind, and self-actualization are mere side products in the search for meaning (p. 9).

Graber (2004) spoke of Frankl's Existential Analysis and Logotherapy, "Its very orientation and motivation, the will to meaning, is based on a sense of responsibility" (p. 18). In other words, as a person discovers meaning in their life, he or she is responsible to reach out to others. Frankl continued on to practice and develop his theory until approximately 1942—where Fabry (1988) says, "[he] tested those ideas during two and a half years in German concentration camps" (p. 1).

So, what does Logotherapy mean? In a nutshell, Logotherapy is the practice of obtaining healing through meaning, or as Fabry said: "Health through meaning" (p. 1). Murasso (2008) wrote that the function of Logotherapy "seeks healing at the spiritual core of man's [humanity's] being. It is at this aspect of man [humanity] that warrants wholeness, because it is at the level of soul that man [humanity] is confronted with his [their] ontology (being)" (p. 19). Logotherapy comes from the two words: Logos, meaning *word*, and therapy, connotes *healing*. Murasso described Logos as "The Second Person of the Blessed Trinity, [and] is revealed as the Incarnate God, the Christ, to those who approach him in pursuit of healing and wholeness" (p. 15). Therefore, in many circles, Logotherapy reflects the works and ministry of Jesus.

The tenets of Logotherapy are self-discovery, choices, uniqueness, responsibility, and self-transcendence. For Frankl, these principles were tested in the German concentration camps. Frankl (1959/2006) wrote the following of himself and his fellow inmates:

> The way in which a man accepts his fate and all the suffering it entails, the way in which he takes up his cross, gives him ample opportunity—even under the most difficult circumstances—to add a deeper meaning to his life. It may remain brave, dignified and unselfish. Or in the bitter fight for self-preservation, he may forget his human dignity and become no more than an animal. Here lies the chance for a man either to make use of or to forgo the opportunities of attaining the moral values that a difficult situation may afford him. And this decides whether he is worthy of his sufferings (p. 7).

As we continue with our discussion of Logotherapy, you will notice that it is often used when challenges come about in one's life. In many cases, there is a disruption in the flow of a person's life (i. e. loss of a job, loss of a loved one, divorce/separation, "mid-life" crisis, a decline in health, etc.). Frankl (1969/1988) spoke of suffering and pain from a Logotherapuetic stance when he said the following: "But what about inescapable suffering? Logotherapy teaches that pain must be avoided as it is possible to avoid it. But as soon as a painful fate cannot be changed, it not only must be accepted but may be transmuted into something meaningful, into an achievement" (p. 72). Regardless of the circumstances, one can find solace in connecting with his or her destiny and meaning. Frankl continued on to say, "the suffering man (person) who, by virtue of his (their) humanness, is capable of rising above, and taking a stand to, his (or her) suffering, moves in a dimension perpendicular to the former" (pp. 74 – 75). In other words, a person who is suffering can face their pain with an attitude that helps them to see their situation in a positive light—the opposite of their current position. However, it is solely dependent upon their attitude. Frankl went on to say:

> A human being strives for success but, if need be, does not depend on his fate, which does or does not *allow* for success. A human being, by the very attitude he chooses, is capable of finding and fulfilling meaning in even a hopeless situation. This fact is understandable only through our dimensional approach, allots to the attitudinal values a higher dimension than to the creative and experiential values. The attitudinal values are the highest possible values (1969/1988, p. 75).

When unavoidable suffering is encountered, the person experiencing the situation will be able to place a higher value on the *meaning* of the situation when their attitude is positive and they are willing to seek the meaning behind that situation. Frankl (1959/2006) beautifully wrote about the meaning of suffering and destiny in the following manner:

> "Life" does not mean something vague, but something very real and concrete, just as life's tasks are also very real and concrete. They form man's destiny, which is different and unique for each individual. No man and no destiny can be compared with any other man or any other destiny. No situation repeats itself, and each situation calls for a different response. Sometimes the situation in which a man finds himself may require him to shape his own fate by action. At other times it is more advantageous for him to make use of an opportunity for contemplation and to realize assets in this way. Sometimes many may be required simply to accept fate, to bear his cross. Every situation is distinguished by its uniqueness, and there is always only one right answer to the problem posed by the situation at hand.
>
> When a man finds that it is his destiny to suffer, he will have to accept his suffering as his task; his single and

unique task. He will have to acknowledge the fact that even in suffering he is unique and alone in the universe. No one can relieve him of his suffering or suffer in his place. His unique opportunity lies in the way in which he bears his burden (p. 77).

Although these words are powerfully eloquent, they speak volumes to the uniqueness of humanity's experiences and the distinctiveness of the individual's life. It also addresses one's need to live and absorb their experiences as opportunities to grow and achieve self-transcendence, even as suffering occurs. It is very important to observe Frankl's emphasis on a person's suffering and the uniqueness of being in that place alone. An individual's suffering is meant to shape them in order to meet their destiny. In other words, distress in one's life is designed to help the individual to be prepared for their God-given work. As Frankl stated, "no one's destiny can be compared to another's." Each person's life and circumstance is different and one of a kind. Therefore, Logotherapy asserts that the person achieves this end in order to help people to attain wholeness through meaning through trying times. Frankl (1959/2006) went on to explain how he and others in the concentration camps arrived at the meaning of their suffering in the following remarks:

What was really needed was a fundamental change in our attitude toward life. We had to learn ourselves and, furthermore, we had to teach the despairing men, that *it did not really matter what we expected from life, but rather what life expected from us.* We needed to stop asking about the meaning of life, and instead to think of ourselves as those who were being questioned by life—daily and hourly, our answer must consist, not in talk and meditation, but right action and in right conduct. Life ultimately means taking the responsibility to find the right answer to its problems and to fulfill the tasks which it constantly sets for each individual (pp. 76 – 77).

<u>Meaning as It Is Meant to Be</u>

In order to bring Logotherapy into a more practical, everyday perspective as it relates to overcoming shame, let's look at the five tenets of Logotherapy as Frankl presented them: 1) self-discovery (will to meaning), 2) choices, 3) uniqueness, 4) responsibility, and 5) self-transcendence. At some points, one may compare Frankl's concepts to those of Abraham H. Maslow (1943) and his "Hierarchy of Needs." Like Frankl, Maslow's Hierarchy of Needs has five areas: physiological needs, need for security, social needs, esteem needs, and self-actualizing needs. Once we continue on discussing Logotherapy we will see how uniquely different these tenets are and why I chose to study Logotherapy closely.

From Frankl's perspective, self-actualization is a limited goal for a person to attain because it only gives him or her material things to strive for without fully satisfying their true quest—meaning in their lives. Frankl (1978) stated that "Self-actualization is possible only as a by-product of self-transcendence" (p. 94). Fabry (1987) also asserted that "Self-actualization is desireable but can be achieved only to the extent to which we fulfill the concrete meaning of a specific situation. If we seek self-actualization for its own sake, we will not attain it" (p. 83). In fact, "Ultimately man [or humanity] can actualize himself only by fulfilling a meaning out in the world, rather than within himself, and self-actualization is available only as an effect of self-transcendence" (Frankl, 1948/1975, p. 95). In Frankl's view, a person who is striving for self-actualization rather than self-transcendence will always be working toward something and not toward their true selves. Frankl (1975) asserted this point of view when he wrote the following:

> I have termed this constitutive characteristic "the self-transcendence of human existence." It denotes the fact that being human always points, and is directed, to something, or someone, other than oneself—be it a meaning to fulfill or another human being to encounter. The more one forgets himself—by giving himself to a cause to serve or another person to love—the more human he is and the more he actualizes himself. what is called self-actualization is not an attainable aim at all, for the simple reason that the more one world strive for it, the more he would miss it. I other words, self-actualization is possible only as a side effect of self-transcendence. (1975, pp. 110 – 111).

In Frankl's *Man's Search for Ultimate Meaning* (2000), he described his treatment of self-discovery, or the will to meaning, and how it plays a crucial role in one's journey towards self-transcendence in that it "denotes the fundamental fact that normally man [people are] is striving to find, and fulfill, meaning and purpose in life" (p. 85). In other words, people try hard to make sense of their lives when faced with situations that challenge what they believe. "Logotherapy expands not only the concept of man [humanity], by including his [their] higher aspirations," Frankl (1978) explained, "but also the visional field of the patient [person] as to potentialities to feed and nurture his [or her] will to meaning... The will to meaning is not only a matter of faith but also a fact" (pp. 30, 31). Take a person who is in a transitional phase of their life, for example. Instead of him or her blaming others or the situation, self-discovery could help them to find the hidden meaning/purpose of their life without being seen in a negative light. "By the same token, Logotherapy immunizes the patient [person] against the dehumanizing, mechanistic concept of man [humanity] on which many a 'shrink' is sold...." (p. 30). A person can find meaning and purpose in their life by becoming motivated to do so. Graber (2004) stated that self-discovery could be enhanced by "Exploring available choices and their potential consequences will serve to enlarge the person's perspective so that the meaning potential of each choice can be seen more clearly" (p. 142). Frankl (1959/2006) also attested:

> Man's search for meaning is the primary motivation in his life and not a "secondary rationalization" of instinctual drives. This meaning is unique and specific in that it must and can be fulfilled by him alone; only then does it achieve a significance which will satisfy his own *will* to meaning... Man, however, is able to live and even to die for the sake of his ideals and values!" (p. 99).

In the course of self-discovery, but not limited to this phase, this process can be hindered by what Frankl (1959/2006) called existential vacuum—where values and inner drives are in conflict (p. 100). The existential vacuum is defined in the following:

> The existential vacuum is in itself not a pathological state. It should be seen as a sign, calling to our attention, that access to the noetic [spiritual] dimension is blocked. Symptoms of the existential vacuum manifest as: doubt, inner emptiness, boredom, lack of initiative, apathy,

nameless dread, conformism, fatalistic thinking, ambivalence, and a sense of existence is meaningless (Graber, 2004, p. 143).

Within self-discovery, the will to meaning portion of one's search for meaning, one must accept the fact that they have a spiritual core—the noetic dimension—of their self. As a person lives, he or she engages in questioning of the reality of life. Murasso (2008) asserted the following explanation:

> Life issues that seek validation by defining life's ultimate concerns are necessarily confronted with that aspect of human existence that defies scientific explanation and at once constitutes a frame of reference for generations of humans... In man's struggle to clearly define the nature and purpose of his human existence, he has generated questions regarding his own immorality, which has generated questions regarding his own ontological dualism and his place in the schema of the universe... Consequently, in his attempt to validate the reality of soul in the trajectory of human existence, man has sought both wholeness and completeness in the world, while at the same time recognizing the propensity to identify with the spiritual, the *noological* (p. 17).

From a Logotherapuetic stance one's healing starts on the spiritual level. As Frankl (1975) said, "human existence is spiritual existence" (p. 26). In other words, a person cannot exist if their spirit is hindered by any means. Therefore, "Logotherapy seeks healing at the spiritual core of man's [humanity's] being. It is this aspect of man [humanity] that warrants wholeness, because it is at the level of soul that man [humanity] is confronted with his ontology..." (Murasso, 2008, p. 19). In essence, the purpose for an individual is to actively participate in the self-discovery process and find worth and meaning in their life. Murasso went further to assert the following:

> In its focus on man's spiritual essence, the *noological* dimension, Logotherapy aims at bringing to man's awareness the spiritual realities. In so doing, the spiritual unconscious becomes conscious through the exchange of words. Through the *logos*, man engages in a process of discernment and self-discovery; thus he can make clear

decisions for his life, leading to a renewed sense of meaning... This self-discovery leads to man's realization that life is worth living and that life holds unconditional value despite the existential dilemmas which confront him. Healing follows when meaning is discovered, leading to a new purpose for living (p. 33).

Once a person begins his or her journey towards self-transcendence, they must be willing to make healthy choices for his or her self. Rooted in existentialism— "objective, universal, and certain knowledge is an unattainable idea"—choices must be based on the person's path not based on outside influences. According to Graber (2004):

> The existentialists conclude, therefore, that human choice is subjective, because individuals finally must make their own choices without help from such external standards as laws, ethical rules, or traditions. Because individuals make their own choices, they are *free*; but because they freely choose, they are completely *responsible* for their choices. The existentialists emphasize that freedom is necessarily accompanied by responsibility (p. 32).

What this is saying is while a person makes choices in his or her life, they should not fragrantly break the law and/or customs, but they should use them and not allow them to dictate their decisions. These choices come from the individual's heart/conscious. Making healthy or appropriate choices appear throughout the other areas of Logotherapy; therefore, I will make mention when necessary.

In discovering and accepting one's uniqueness, Frankl (1959/2006) stated, "Everyone has his [or her] own specific vocation or mission in life to carry out a concrete assignment which demands fulfillment. Therein he [or she] cannot be replaced, nor can his [or her] life be repeated. Thus, everyone's task is as unique as is his specific opportunity to implement it" (p. 109). Really, this statement sums self-discovery up concisely. However, Frankl continued to say,

> As each situation in life represents a challenge to man and presents a problem for him to solve, the question of the meaning of life may actually be reversed. Ultimately, man

should not ask what the meaning of his life is, but rather he must recognize that it is *he* who is asked. In other words, each man is questioned by life; and he can only answer to life by answering for his own life; to life he can only respond by being responsible...." (p. 109).

In other words, your meaning and/or purpose in life is solely yours. No one can perform the task set before *you* nor can *you* perform anyone else's. Fabry (1988) succinctly hit the nail on the proverbial head, so to speak, when he wrote:

> The search for meaning through uniqueness is different from the one that leads to the 'aha' experiences of self-discovery. Your uniqueness becomes evident not so much as by what you are as by how important you are in relationships with other people or situations (p. 67).

What you bring to the relationship or situation is uniquely you, not an imitation of someone or something else— "...each person is unique, going through a lifelong series of unique, unrepeatable moments, each offering a meaning potential..." (Fabry, 1968/1987, p. 18). To be sure, Fabry described Frankl's sense of uniqueness in the following manner:

> Meaning is "what is meant," he says, meant for you, in your present situation. It is specific, unique, and personal. You cannot take someone else's meaning or recover the meaning of a situation once it is past. Life and its string of meanings keep rolling along. That is the basis for the logotherapeutic tenet that each person is unique—we live our unique life, have our unique opportunities, potentials, and shortcomings. We create unique relationships and accept unique tasks, face unique sufferings, experience unique guilt feelings, and die a unique death. The search for meaning is highly personal and distinct (p. 54).

The next tenet, responsibility, influences the other aforementioned areas, which undergirds self-transcendence in Logotherapy. Graber (2004) astutely noted:

> The existentialists emphasize that freedom is necessarily accompanied by responsibility. Furthermore, since individuals are forced to choose for themselves, they have

their freedom, and therefore their responsibility, thrust upon them. They are "condemned to be free." They insist that individuals must accept full responsibility for their behavior, no matter how difficult. If an individual is to live meaningfully and *authentically*, he or she must become fully aware of the true character of the human situation and bravely accept it (p. 32).

As one lives a meaning-filled life, he or she must do so responsibly—living productively while being mindful of others as well as themselves. Fabry (1988) wisely said,

> We *want* to find meaning by personal choices that express our true and unique selves. But if those choices are not made responsibly, they will not be fulfilling. Just as pleasure without meaning is empty, and power without purpose is corrupting, so choice without responsibility is meaningless (p. 79).

Now we have arrived at the most important tenet of Logotherapy, self-transcendence—to move beyond yourself. Frankl (1978) in his monumental work, *The Unheard Cry for Meaning*, explained:

> I thereby understand the primordial anthropological fact that being human is being always directed, and pointing, to something or someone other than oneself: to a meaning to fulfill or another human being to encounter, a cause to serve or a person to love. Only to the extent that someone is living out this self-transcendence of human existence, is he truly human or does he become his true self. He becomes so, not by concerning himself with his self's actualization, but by forgetting himself and giving himself, overlooking himself and focusing outward (p. 35).

Frankl (1975) continued on to iterate this concept of self-transcendence in his *The Unconscious God*:

> Thus, human existence is always directed to something, or someone, other than itself—be it a meaning to fulfill or another human being to encounter lovingly. I have termed this constitutive characteristic of human existence "self-transcendence." What is called "self-actualization" is

ultimately an effect, the unintentional by-product, of self-transcendence... Therefore, man is originally characterized by his "search for meaning" rather than his "search for himself." The more one forgets himself—giving oneself to a cause or another person—the more *human* he is. And the more one is immersed and absorbed in something or someone other than oneself the more he really becomes *himself* (pp. 78, 79).

Frankl (1978) commented on the intentionality of transcending the self and cautioned us of its rejection when he wrote:

> The self-transcendent quality of the human reality in turn is reflected in the "intentional" quality of human phenomena... When the self-transcendence of existence is denied, existence itself is distorted. It is reified. Being is reduced to a mere thing. Being human is de-personalized. And, what is most important, the subject is made into an object. This is due to the fact that it is the characteristic of a subject that it relates to intentional objects in terms of values and meanings which serve as reasons and motives. If self-transcendence is denied and the door to meanings and values is closed, reasons and motives are replaced by conditioning processes, and it is up to the "hidden persuaders" to do the conditioning, to manipulate man. It is reification that opens the door to manipulation (pp. 52 – 53).

Meant to Move Forward

Logotherapy has many ways of helping people to achieve wholeness through meaning, and, thus, reaching self-transcendence. However, in this context, two methods will be presented as ways to manage and/or overcome shame: De-reflection and paradoxical intentions. In Logotherapy, "De-reflection is intended to counteract compulsive inclination to self-observation" (Fabry et al., 1979, p. 85). Frankl (1968/1987) explained de-reflection in the following manner:

> It is applicable in cases where the symptom results from "hyper-reflection" or "hyperintentention," where the problem is caused by excessive attention given to a normal

bodily function. ...Here again a pattern developed and has to be broken, and again it makes little difference how it started (pp. 141 – 142).

In this way, a person is called to look at themselves in a positive light, rather than scrutiny and judgment. De-reflection flies in the face of the old saying, "You are your worse critic." Take Cissy, for example, who maintained an immaculate home in order to keep the appearance of being a "proper" mother and wife. Instead of cleaning obsessively whenever she felt that she was not living up to par, she could learn to do something relaxing for herself. In this same instance, it would not be necessary for Cissy to brood over what she was not doing or could be doing to show her worth. Cissy can view her behavior in a way that could lead to a life beyond the walls of her home and herself.

Using logotherapy could help a person dealing with shame to trust themselves again. In many of Frankl inserts regarding de-reflection, he spoke of an artist or a musician. I believe it can also be applicable in this context as well. In his book, *The Unconscious God*, Frankl (1975) wrote:

> Therapy had to start with eliminating this tendency to overbearing self-reflection and self-observance, or in the terminology of logotherapy, "hyper-reflection." Therapy had to be aimed at what we call in logotherapy "de-reflection." Treatment had to give back to the patient [person] his trust in the unconscious, by having him realize how much more musical his unconscious was than his conscious. as a matter of fact, this treatment oriented toward the release of the artistic "creative powers: of his unconscious. De-reflection liberated the creative process from the inhibiting effects of any unnecessary reflection (p. 38).

Therefore, in the case of Cissy, as you may recall, she was a Certified Public Accountant by trade. She became a homemaker by her husband's insistence and began feeling as though she was not living her life to its fullest potential. De-reflection could help Cissy by having her to trust her abilities as a homemaker and as an accountant if she chooses to return to her profession.

The next method is paradoxical intention. Frankl

(1969/1988) stated that "Paradoxical intention means that the patient [person] is encouraged to do, or wish to happen, the very things he [or she] fears" (p. 102). In using paradoxical intention, the person is assisted in identifying their fears and what they would do if they were not afraid. Frankl (1978) clearly described this concept in the following manner:

> To understand how paradoxical intention works, take as a starting point the mechanism called anticipatory anxiety: a given symptom evokes on the part of the patient [person] the fearful expectation that it might recur. Fear, however, always tends to bring about precisely that which is feared, and by the same token, anticipatory anxiety is liable and likely to trigger off what the patient so fearfully expects to happen. Thus, a self-sustaining vicious circle is established.... ...this is precisely the business to accomplish by paradoxical intention, which may be defined as a process by which *the patient is encouraged to do, or to wish to happen, the very things he fears...* (pp. 115, 117, emphasis mine).

One feature of paradoxical intention is the use of humor. It allows a person to step away and look at themselves from the outside to realize how humorous their shortcomings may be. Fabry (1987) stated that "It can also be tried with persons who want to change unwanted behavior patterns: stuttering, blushing, sweating, sleeplessness, or the fear of forgetting lines when making public appearances" (p. 137). Tweedie (1961) asserted the following regarding the role of humor in paradoxical intention:

> The role of humor in this logotherapeutic technique is very important. Nothing is so effective in putting distance between a person and his [or her] problem as a humorous experience. The patient [person] almost invariably laughs when he [or she] first hears, and first attempts to carry out, the instruction of paradoxical intention. The therapist should utilize this situation as much as possible, for it is an important medium of psychonoetic antagonism. When the patient [person] is able to laugh at his [or her] anxieties, he [or she] is on the road to improvement. ...Frankl believes that humor is a unique existential capacity of man [humanity], and an excellent mode of self detachment (p. 114).

Humor also serves as the ice breaker and releases the person to "loosen up," for lack of better words. Fabry (1987) further elucidated:

> Patients [people] learn to apply paradoxical intention *before* they are caught in the feared situation, at a time when they still can concentrate on formulating their phrases. They learn to phrase their formulations as true intentions ('I'll show my boss how much I can sweat!'), not as anticipation ('I'm not going to sweat!') because anticipation only deepens the fear (pp. 138 – 139).

Using paradoxical intention with persons who displays shame-filled body language, for example, can be ideal. A young woman, who is ashamed of a part of her body, may react shamefully when given a compliment. Her immediate reaction may be her crossing her arms across her chest or pulling her blouse/shirt down or up. On some levels of her unconscious mind, her response may be an indication of how she feels, what she had been told, or what may have been the center of negative attention in her past, which is shown in her body language. This young woman may not be aware of her "wanting cover up or disappear" body language; however, if phrased in a way that is humorous, she may be able to laugh at her own behavior and realize that she should be proud of how God made her.

In conclusion, Logotherapy not only centers on individuals finding wholeness through meaning, but it is drawn from logos, "the Second Person of the Blessed Trinity" (Murraso, 2008), Jesus the Christ. Murraso also succinctly noted:

> Christ as *Logos* did for the wounded, the blind, the lepers and the lame what practitioners of Logotherapy attempt to do for their clients: reawaken the bruised and buried human spirit by helping man to discover and to cultivate meaning and purpose in his life (p. 16).

When an individual discovers that his or her life has meaning, and that the situations in their lives are meant for the service of humanity and the up-building of the Kingdom of God, he or she will be able to recognize the significance of their lives as unique beings. Logotherapy, if applied appropriately, can abolish the crippling effects of shame and convert the lived experiences into ministry for those suffering from challenging circumstances in their lives. As Romans 8: 28 declares: "And we know that God causes everything to work together for the good of those who love God and are called according to his purpose for them" (*NLT*). Through Logotherapy, one can arrive at a full understanding of God's intent for their life.

Part Four:
Making Sense of it All

"After breakfast Jesus said to Simon Peter, 'Simon son of John, do you love me more than these?' 'Yes, Lord,' Peter replied, 'you know I love you.' 'Then feed my lambs,' Jesus told him. Jesus repeated the question: 'Simon son of John, do you love me?' 'Yes Lord,' Peter said, 'you know I love you.' 'Then take care of my sheep,' Jesus said. Once more he asked him, 'Simon son of John, do you love me?' Peter was grieved that Jesus asked the question a third time. He said, 'Lord, you know everything. You know I love you.' Jesus said, 'Then feed my sheep. The truth is, when you were young, you were able to do as you liked and go wherever you wanted to. But when you are old, you will stretch out your hands, and others will direct you and take you where you don't want to go.' Jesus said this to let him know what kind of death he would die to glorify God. Then Jesus told him, 'Follow me.'"

John 21: 15 – 19 (*New Living Translation*)

"For I am not ashamed of this Good News about Christ. It is the power of God at work, saving everyone who believes—the Jew first and also the Gentile."

Acts 17: 28 – 29 (*New Living Translation*)

In naming this last section, *Making Sense of It All*, it was not intended to create a false sense of an exhaustive grasp of our lives—what will happen, how it will happen and when it will happen. It is a declaration of faith. Yet at the same time, it speaks to the ongoing collaborative relationship we have with God and others. The Bible says, "A man's [or woman's] mind plans his [or her] way, but the Lord directs his [or her] steps and makes them sure" (Proverbs 16: 9, *AMB*). God graciously gives us the gift of free will to which we should freely turn over to God. Therefore, our role is to seek God for God's path and direction in our lives.

Writing this book was a great labor of my heart because I was able to get a glimpse of God's desire to free me from a lot of things I have been trying to hide and avoid for far too long. You see, when I spoke of how shame can hinder us, I am a living witness. When I completed my doctoral dissertation and traveled to Florida to attend my commencement ceremony, all types of emotions swirled around in my heart and in my mind. One of the main feelings was that my achievement, although it was huge, superseded those of my parents. Sure, that is the goal: children should achieve higher heights than their parents. Yet it did not feel good in that moment. I believe this was compounded by the fact that both my dad (Charles L. Anderson) and my father (Curtis B. Calloway) were not physically present. However, I took solace in my belief that they were with me in spirit. I had accomplished what they wanted me to all the while, but I felt a sense of incompleteness in my heart.

Once my doctoral process was completed and its celebratory events took place and became memories, it took some time for me to pick up a book, let alone write something to this extent. I slowly began to realize what God had done in my life to which invigorated my sense of direction. First, I was able to rest, and then, I was able to enter a season where I had to be poured into in order to pour into others. This book is the first major portion of this "pouring out" season. And by doing so, this project reminded me of the information I was blessed to have been exposed to, and it allowed me to see my calling anew—Youth Pastor and Christian Counselor/Therapist. I was able to realize how much our youths are suffering and in search for relief—or direction. I feel more confident through Christ to boldly step forth and POUR INTO those with whom I come into contact with in some way.

My hope for us all is that we will learn and continue to seek God's counsel and learn more about God's plan for us as we travel on the road of managing and overcoming the shame in of lives. Reflecting on the meaning of shame for a moment we will find, in the simplest of terms, the function of shame "reveals the inner self, exposing it to view" (Kaufman, 1996, p. 17). In my opinion, shame causes us to think we, ourselves, or someone can see us for who we are, which incites feelings of inadequacies, insecurities and unworthiness. We continue on trying to hide ourselves from others, wishing we can either disappear altogether or at least that part of our being we so despise will go away. But it does not go away because it is a part of our life stories, our testimonies. Rest assured that God sees all. God loves us so much that God is willing and able to forgive our sins when we humbly pray for forgiveness and repent from the sin that caused the shame, whether it be our own doing or by the hands of others. This may not make sense to you right now, because you may believe your shame is too big or so deep. You have to be willing to ask the question: Is there anything too big for my God to solve? And then, you have to believe the answer is unequivocally: There is nothing too big, too hard for my God to solve.

I pray that this book will speak to your heart and initiate change and growth. Although I do understand that this in and of itself is not the last word regarding shame, my hope is that it will spark an awareness of your need for healing and redirection, which could only be achieved through the Word of God and God's love. As you have prayerfully read and contemplated the things written in this book, you might have seen God's manifestations, because honestly, most of it was not my doing. It was my fingers that typed, but after reading the words myself, I saw that it was God's handiwork. So, go in the peace of knowing that we have a Comforter who will never leave nor abandon us. Jesus promised "And surely I am with you always, to the very end of the age" (Matthew 28: 20b, *NIV*).

One last note, God has given us many tools and abilities to live an abundant life, even in the midst of pain and struggles. As we live, we will make mistakes and will be mistreated at times. But God wants us to be able to forgive and show compassion toward others, and ourselves. Your initial desire might be to hold a grudge, retaliate, and even hate others for what they have done to you. You might go as far as blaming yourself for allowing yourself to be mistreated or taken advantage of in the first place. Sadly, this behavior may create a pattern of condemnation and lack of compassion that will become difficult to change. But God desires for us to forgive ourselves and others, regardless of what the situation may be. When you do not forgive yourself and others it is extremely hard to show compassion to them and yourself. This is where cynical and contemptible attitudes begin and grow. We all must do as Jesus taught in John 13: "A new commandment I give to you, that you love one another; even as I have loved you, that you also love one another" (v. 34, *Revised Standard*). In doing so, forgiveness and compassion are some of its fruits.

In closing, allow me to leave you with a portion from *A Tale of Three Kings: A Study in Brokenness*. Its words speak of ways in which we can choose to be freed from shame and limitations forced upon our lives. The Prologue of this powerful little book starts with the following phrase: "The Almighty, living God turned to Gabriel and gave a command" (Edwards, 1992, p. xvii). God wanted Gabriel to go on a mission to give "two unborn destinies" to give them something special— "two portions of my being" (p. xvii). Below you will find the words Gabriel spoke onto the two unborn destinies:

> A destiny stepped forward: "This portion of God is for me." "True," replied the angel. "And remember, whoever receives such a great portion of power will surely be known by many. Ere your earthly pilgrimage is done, your true character will be known; yea, it will be *revealed* by means of this power. Such is the destiny of all who want and wield this portion, for it touches only the outer person, affecting the inner person not one whit. Outer power will always unveil the inner resources or the lack thereof."
>
> Gabriel spoke again. "I have here the second of two elements of the living God. This is not a gift but an inheritance. A gift is worn on the outer person; an inheritance is planted deep inside—like a seed. Yet, even though it is such a small planting, this planting grows segment and, in time, fills all the inner person." Another destiny steeped forward. "I believe this element is to be mine for my earthly pilgrimage." "True," responded the

angel again. "I must tell you that what has been given to you is a glorious thing—the only element in the universe that can change the human heart. Yet even this element of God cannot accomplish its task nor grow and fill your entire inner being unless it is compounded will. It must be mixed lavishly with pain, sorrow, and crushing" (pp. xviii – xix).

Go in the peace of God knowing that God has predestined you to travel on your journey called life. Blesses be unto you.

Epilogue

Working on this book has been a powerfully moving experience for me. *No Shame* has opened my eyes to many things that I refused to see before working on this project. As I researched and worked on this book, I prayed for God to show me some things that needed cleaning up and working out in my life. Once this project was done, I discovered that God was not finished with me in regard to shame and writing about it. So, I prayed for a clearer vision as to what I would write about and whom the next book would address. Some time had passed and I moved on, almost forgetting about the follow up to *No Shame*. And then, something happened that brought this subject back into focus. My younger sister, Tihira, and I were talking about future goals, when she suggested that I a book about the type of therapy I felt called to practice. That was powerful because Tihira's input convinced me to pursue my doctorate degree. I admitted to her that day, "I still haven't fully dealt with my stuff." Because Tihira is aware of what that "stuff" means, she encouraged me to write anyhow "because writing brings you peace and it will give you chance to work out some of your stuff and give you a clearer idea of what you are supposed to do." Now that was wisdom and I was proud of her.

I continued to pray for direction and got into position to listen to what God had for me to hear. I had to go to a spiritual place where I can receive guidance and clarity because writing on this subject matter, which I knew would be emotionally taxing on me. I decided I would devote some time praying and thinking about this while I was away from home in the summer of 2013. By this time, I had been reading about various biblical characters, looking for inspiration. I did so in haste because I wanted to get started and approach this work on my own terms. I spent chunks of time during the day searching for something. I started reading *No Shame*, hoping that something would jump out. Nothing happened; and nothing jumped out.

It appeared that God remind me that I had to be patient and wait on him. This continued until one day I spent quality time with my mentee, who I will call little grasshopper. Little grasshopper has a sweet spirit and is a loving person but was in desperate need of guidance and positive influences in their life. Most importantly, little grasshopper could really benefit from seeing a strong Black man doing positive things and sharing love with them that does not require or was not accompanied by shame. Well, on this particular day, while interacting with little grasshopper, I came in close contact with old feelings of shame. It startled me to the point where I had to pray ask the Lord where they came from, "because I got over those things and I don't wanna back, again." Unbeknownst to me, that is what I had to do—go back. I found a way to "get over" some of experiences without dealing them. But God has a way of humbling us when our arrogance and pride comes into play. I had to go back, mentally and emotionally, to see that I needed this project just as much as someone else does, especially little grasshopper. That is when God took me to the title and the focus of my next book, entitled, *Tamar's Healing*.

When I received this word for the Lord, I thought it did not make sense because, according to the biblical account, Tamar never "got over" what happened to her. So, I prayed for clarity again, and that was the point—she did not get over what happened to her because the Word (Jesus) had not become flesh to be slain for the sins of the world. Once I openly received God's direction, I was able to see that my goal for the follow up book, *Tamar's Healing*, was to be specifically geared toward abuse and shame. As I write these words, I am also working on *Tamar's Healing*. I have to say God is doing some powerful things because when I proofread various sections, I find myself either scratching my chin in amazement or I shed tears because I felt God's hand is moving in my life. Through the words on the pages, I found that God's loving hope still abounds as God's seeks to restore his people.

Dr. Kasim Ali Sidney Jones

     I invite and encourage you to also read *Tamar's Healing* to receive God's love to heal some areas of your life that you may have denied for far too long. I believe God wants to use each and every one of us for God's glory. It is our testimonies that reach those lost in this sin sick world. God bless you.

December 3, 2013

No Shame in the Game

About the Author

Reverend Doctor Kasim Ali Sidney Jones was born on October 11, 1971 to Reverend Shirley A. Jones and the late Curtis B. Calloway in Belleville, New Jersey, and was reared by the late Charles L. Anderson. He grew up in East Orange, NJ, where he was the youngest of four boys—Willie III, Roy, Sr., and Duane. In 1990, he became the proud "big brother" of Tihira S. Jones-Anderson, and Roy and Connie Anderson followed thereafter. Dr. Jones received his primary and secondary education in the East Orange School System to which he graduated from East Orange High School in June of 1991. He attended Essex County College in Newark, N. J. and transferred to Kean University (formerly Kean College in Union, N. J.), where he earned a Bachelor of Social Work degree in 1999. Dr. Jones relocated to Atlanta, GA in the summer of 1999 to study at the Interdenominational Theological Center and earned a Master of Divinity degree in Psychology of Religion and Pastoral Care. Dr. Jones studied at Argosy University in Sarasota, FL, where he earned a Doctor of Education degree in Pastoral Community Counseling. Finally, on May 3, 2003, Rev. Dr. Jones was ordained as a Minister of the Gospel of Jesus Christ by the Chapel of Christian Love Missionary Baptist Church and the Mount Calvary Baptist Association (Atlanta, Georgia).

Dr. Jones has worked with and advocated for youths for over 20 years. Since his teens, he has been a confidant to a number of his peers as they struggled with familial and personal issues. Dr. Jones volunteered at various agencies and shelters in the Newark, New Jersey area throughout the 1990s. He mentored several teens that have reached adulthood and pursued their dreams in various ways. Dr. Jones is a firm believer in the example of Jesus Christ when he reached out to others and helped them to see and pursue their purpose for their lives.

Dr. Jones continued on to pursue his passion professionally by earning a BSW and other levels of learning and begun his career by working with young adults with emotional and psychological challenges. In the spring of 1999, Dr. Jones acknowledged his calling into the Counseling Ministry. He began studying Psychology of Religion/ Pastoral Counseling at the Interdenominational Theological Center in August of that same year. He began attending the Chapel of Christian Love Baptist, under the leadership of Reverend Doctor James Allen Milner, Sr., soon after arriving in Atlanta. While doing so, Dr. Jones completed a Chaplain Residency at Grady Memorial Hospital and worked in the Youth Department of the Chapel of Christian Love and later became the Youth Pastor. Dr. Jones also worked in various secular capacities where he was able to contribute to the wellbeing of children and youth and their families. Dr. Jones eventually went on to earn his doctorate from Argosy University. Dr. Jones is a Board-Certified Pastoral Counselor/Therapist (GA), Clinician/Therapist (GA), and former Youth Pastor (Chapel of Christian Love Baptist, Atlanta, GA).

References

Allender, D. B. (2008). *The wounded heart: Hope for adult victims of childhood sexual abuse: Includes information on false memory issues.* Colorado Springs, CO: NavPress.

Allport, G. W. (1975). *The nature of prejudice* (25th ann. ed.). New York: Basic Books.

Barclay, W. (1975). *The gospel of John: The daily study Bible Series (Vol. 1, rev. ed.).* Philadelphia: The Westminster Press.

Bradshaw, J. ((1990). *Family secrets: The path from shame to healing.* New York: Bantam Books.

Branson, B. and Silva, P. J. (2007). *Violence among us: Ministry to families in crisis.*

Costello, R. B. (Ed.). (1997). The *American heritage college dictionary* (3rd. ed.). Boston: Houghton Mifflin Company.

Edwards, G. (1980/1992). *A tale of three kings: A study in brokenness.* Carol Stream, IL: Tysdale House Publishers, Inc.

Fabry, J. B. (1968/1987). *The pursuit of meaning: Viktor Frankl, logotherapy, and life* (new rev. ed.). Berkley, CA: Institute of Logotherapy Press.

_____ (1988). *Guideposts to meaning: Discovering what really matters.* Oakland, CA: New Harbinger Publications.

Frankl, V. E. (1948/1975). *The unconscious God.* New York: Washington Square Press.

_____ (1948/2000). *Man's search for ultimate meaning.* New York: Basic Book.

_____ (1955/1980). *The doctor and the soul: From psychotherapy to logotherapy* (rev. and expanded ed.). New York: Vintage Books.

_____ (1959/2006). *Man's search for meaning.* Boston: Beacon Press.

_____ (1969/1988). *The will to meaning: Foundations and applications of logotherapy* (expanded ed.). New York: A Meridian Book.

_____ (1978). *The unheard cry for meaning: Psychotherapy & Humanism.* New York, NY: Simon and Schuster.

Graber, A. V. (2004). *Viktor Frankl's logotherapy: Method of choice in ecumenical pastoral psychology* (2nd ed.).

Hawkins, D. R. (1995/2002). *Power vs. force: The hidden*

determinants of human behavior. Carlsbad, CA: Hay house, Inc.

The HarperCollins Study Bible: New Revised Standard Version with the Apocryphal/Deuteroncanonical Books (1993). New York, N. Y.: HarperCollinsPublishers.

The Holy Bible: New International Version (1996). Grand Rapids, Michigan: Zondervan.

Kaufman, G. (1989/1996). *The psychology of shame: Theory and treatment of shame-based syndromes* (2nd ed.). New York, NY: Springer Publishing Company.

Lewis, M. (1992/1995). *Shame: The exposed self*. New York: The Free Press.

McKim. D. K. (1996). *Westminster dictionary of theological terms*. Louisville, KT: Westminster John Knox Press.

The Message: The Bible in Contemporary Language (2002). Colorado Springs, Colorado: Navpress.

Moloney, F. J. (1998). *The gospel of John*. Collegeville, MN: The Liturgical Press.

Murasso, J. N. (2008). *Logotherapy and the logos of God in Christic wisdom*. Belleville, Ontario, Canada: Guardian Books.

Tweedie, D. F., Jr. (1961). *Logotherapy and the Christian faith: An evaluation of Frankl's existential approach to psychotherapy.* Grand Rapids: Baker Book House.

Wilson, S. D. (1990). *Released from shame: Recovery for adult children of dysfunctional families.* Downers Grove, IL: People Helper Books.

Wimberly, E. P. (1997). *Recalling our own stories: Spiritual renewal for religious caregivers.* San Francisco: Jossey-Bass Publishers.

_____ (1999). *Moving from shame to self-worth: Preaching and pastoral care.* Nashville: Abingdon Press.

www.ingramcontent.com/pod-product-compliance
Lightning Source LLC
Chambersburg PA
CBHW072208100526
44589CB00015B/2422